SUCCESS

SUCCESS

HOW TO BE
CALM, CONFIDENT & FOCUSED.

BEN BERNSTEIN, PH.D.
PERFORMANCE COACH

helping families be happy

Note to the reader:
This book is intended to be informational and should not be considered a substitute for advice or therapeutic counseling from a professional psychologist, who should be consulted by the reader in all matters related to his or her psychological health and particularly with regard to any symptoms that may require diagnosis and treatment.

Published by Familius LLC, www.familius.com

Familius books are available at special discounts for bulk purchases for sales promotions, family or corporate use. Special editions, including personalized covers, excerpts of existing books, or books with corporate logos, can be created in large quantities for special needs. For more information, contact Premium Sales by emailing specialmarkets@familius.com

Library of Congress Catalog-in-Publication Data
2013933821

pISBN 978-1-938301-18-6
eISBN 978-1-938301-17-9

Printed in the United States of America

Cover design by Kurt Wahlner
Book design by Kurt Wahlner
Cover photo courtesy Eliot Khuner Photography

10 9 8 7 6 5 4 3 2 1

First Edition

Contents

Dedication

For every teenager who seeks to live a meaningful life.
This book is dedicated to you and your journey.

Appreciations

My beloved teacher, Viola Spolin, once said, "We learn through experience and experiencing and no one teaches anyone anything." She meant that the only way we truly learn is by *doing*. A teacher doesn't "teach" as much as create an environment for each person to be actively involved, and through that action, to learn. Spolin showed me that the possibilities for learning are infinite and ever-present when we open ourselves up to them. In my work, each day, I encounter people of different ages and backgrounds, and through every interaction I learn—about them, about myself, and about being human.

In addition to Spolin, I am ever grateful to my teachers whose gifts continue to bear fruit: Catherine Shainberg, Colette Aboulker-Muscat, Wendla Kernig, and David E. Hunt, and to my spiritual guides whose teachings I practice daily on my path.

I am thankful to all the teenagers and families I have worked with and what they've shown me about the daily struggles we all face when we want to live a healthy, fulfilling life. I am grateful to a number of individuals who have contributed specifically to the creation of this book: Candace Lazarou, Andrea I. Jepson, Bonnie Buckner, Judy Rosenfeld, Sharon Goldinger, Fritz Streiff, Jeff Louie; to Maggie Wickes and to all the teens in Huntsville, Utah who gave of their time and energy to look at their common challenges. Thanks to Kurt Wahlnner for the cover and book design. Great appreciateionfor Sam McConkie for his copy editing. I am particularly thankful to Christopher and Michele Robbins, the publishers of this book, for their extraordinary dedication and their obvious love for what they are doing, the people they work with, and their beautiful family.

I drafted the manuscript for this book during an extended stay at vaidyagrama, an Ayurvedic healing village in Tamil Nadu, India. The love, care, and compassion of the doctors and staff and the environment they create gave me the space and opportunity to be grounded and contemplative as I dove into this material. I thank them deeply for what they give. I hope their mission and message reach many people around the world.

Every morning when I wake up I say a prayer of thanks for my family, for my friends, for the gifts I have been given, for my spiritual teachers who guide me on this path, and for my wife, as we move, side-by-side, into the place of more and more light. Her support is my greatest blessing.

My life is a daily lesson in how to be more calm, confident, and focused. I am grateful to you, the reader, for considering with me how rich our possibilities are.

This Book is Yours

As I complete this book, my wife and I are in southern India. We are staying in a quiet place, far from the tumult of the cities. The sun is rising and brightly colored birds are chirping loudly. I am looking out on a wide expanse of banana trees. Their big, bright green leaves are soaking up the warm penetrating rays of the sun.

I am remembering a conversation I had at home, in California, with a friend of mine, a nurse at a local high school. "A lot of students come into my office," she said, "just to talk about life. When I ask them, 'What makes a good life, a happy life?' they often start out saying 'A big house. Lots of money.' But then I ask them, 'So what if you've got all that. Then what? Or what if you don't have all that? Can you still have a good life?'

When we peel away the usual, commercial ideas of what's good and successful, they all want the same thing: they want to be useful, they want to serve, to fall in love, to have a family, to be creative. They basically believe in a deep core of goodness. Even though they're often insecure and question everything, they know they're good. They want a fulfilling life, a satisfying life."

I wish that you, dear reader, could walk out onto this veranda and sit with me, and we could talk about your life. As our conversation deepens, the sun will continue to climb, and the heat will grow more intense. And then, as it grows later, the air will cool and the shadows will lengthen. As you get up to leave I'll hand you this book and say, "This is for you. Use it well."

Outside Coimbatore, south India.
February 2013

CHAPTER 1

Becoming Yourself

You Have a Lot Going On

Lots of homework, your friends are texting you, your parents are on your case, you have to go to practice (piano, football, ballet, you name it), your Facebook page is out of date, you wish you could *go* on a date, you don't have enough friends, your SAT scores are too low, your college applications are late, no one wants to go to the prom with you, your parents won't let you use the car, your teachers don't have a clue of how much work you have to do, you feel bad about the kid who is being bullied, your face is breaking out, and you're totally sleep deprived.

How can you manage it all? How can you possibly succeed?

Calm, Confident, and Focused

In this book I'm going to give you the three keys to being successful. You already know them from the book's subtitle so my cards are on the table. When you learn—really learn—to be calm, confident, and focused—you'll be amazed at how much you can handle and not just handle but do really *well*. You'll be able to succeed in all kinds of ways: in school, on tests, in sports, on stage, with your friends, with your parents, your siblings, and in a part-time job (if you have one). *Being calm, remaining confident, and staying focused are the three keys to success in any endeavor of life.*

How do I know this? I've been a psychologist for thirty-five years and my area of specialization is *success* and how people become successful. To figure this out I've studied, observed, and coached people in many fields—sports, business, teaching, healthcare, the performing arts, to name a few—and over and over again I've seen that there is a foundation that every successful person has built. Laying this foundation doesn't depend on their circumstances— whether they have lived a less-than-privileged life or if they were given a better lot at birth. It doesn't matter if people have "talent" or not. It doesn't even matter if they have failed many times. What matters is this: that they have learned how to be calm, confident, and focused.

Here's an example of what I'm talking about:

Shauna and Dave are both high school juniors and are in the same math class. Today is the day of their mid-term exam. Shauna had a study schedule and stuck with it. She asked her teacher questions and sought out friends who understood parts of the material better. She got a good night's sleep and had breakfast. Dave, however, was up until 3:00 am cramming and downing a big cup of coffee on his way to school. He didn't prepare much, preferring to hang out with his friends. Now Shauna and Dave are sitting down at their desks to take the test. Dave is a bundle of nerves. His legs are bobbing up and down as he anxiously waits while the teacher hands out the exam. Shauna closes her eyes briefly to take a deep breath and center herself. The first problem stumps Dave. His heart starts pounding and his mind spins out, "I've never seen this before!" It's all downhill from there. He struggles through but when he has another tough question he gives up, thinking, "I'm not going to pass." Shauna methodically works through each problem. When she has one that's unfamiliar she slows herself down and reminds herself "I can figure this out," and goes step-by-step with what she does know until she solves the problem. Dave is so distracted by the thoughts that he is going to fail he doesn't finish the test. Shauna stays focused—on track—and has a few minutes to review a couple of uncertain answers.

Simply put, Shauna is calm, confident, and focused. Dave is not.

We've all seen people at the top of their game—championship athletes, rock stars, and successful business CEOs—and we know what that looks like. As the Olympic gymnast prepares to do her vault, as the rock star looks out into the stadium filled with 20,000 people, as the executive seals the deal for fifty million dollars, what they all have in common is this: they are calm, confident, and focused.

I know, these people have talent and they work really hard. But that's not why they're successful. I'm talking about something even more basic. I'm talking about the platform for success which *everyone* shares. I'm talking about what they do with their talent and what is actually going on when they practice, prepare, and when they perform. What you see, over and over, is that they all use the same three keys: they've learned to be calm, confident, and focused, and they've practiced using these keys so they are second nature.

You can learn to use these keys. You too can be successful.

What Is Success?

Nearly everyone moans about how hard the teenage years are. Teenagers moan, parents moan, teachers moan. I've heard some parents say they wish there was a planet their kids could go to when they become teenagers and then come back to earth when those years have passed. But I have a different take. I think that as challenging and chaotic as these years can be—and they often are—they can also be the most exciting, rewarding, and growth-producing time of your young life.

Why do I say this? Because *you are on the threshold of your future and all of your possibilities*. You have the chance, now, to prepare yourself in the right way. This is the time when you are growing into your best and brightest self. While this might not make sense to you right now, and may even seem a little scary, I can assure you that as you learn and use the tools I'm giving you in this book these years will become much more an adventure than an endurance contest for you and for everyone in your life. As you experience success now—and not have to wait until you're "grown up"—your world will open up, right now. Rather than feel like life is just *too much* and you want to pull the covers over your head—and who doesn't sometimes?—you will take on the challenges of being and becoming yourself, knowing that you are growing and blossoming.

Let's pause for a moment and consider what I mean by "success." Conventionally, the word conjures up a pile of money, a fabulous car, a big house, the ability to travel, and having lots of *things*. While there's nothing wrong with any of this, what I mean by "success" is actually much deeper and more lasting. To me, success means being happy. It means feeling fulfilled. If you're thinking, "Well, I'd be happy with a Ferrari!" I won't argue with you. I'd be happy with one, too. But *lasting* happiness never came from owning a great car or from having a lot of money or from good looks. It comes from owning yourself. It comes from being fully you.

As you read that last sentence you may have been thinking, "Ugh. He doesn't get it. I really don't like myself. I'm not as [handsome, beautiful, rich, talented—choose your adjective] as [Susie, LeVon, Ming, Scott—name the person]. All that may be true. But saying "I'm not this" or "I'm not that" just gets you tied up in NOTS (excuse the pun). You aren't giving any positive attention to who you *are*. The truth is you will *never* be like Susie, LeVon, Ming, or Scott. Why? Because you're *you*. You might as well accept and like who *you* are. Stop fighting, stop whining, and get with your own program. Unless you do—and until you do—you're not going to be happy.

Let Me Tell You a Story . . .

I'll tell you how I first discovered this. When I was a boy growing up in Brooklyn, New York in the 1950s I didn't like the way I looked. I had a skinny body and a big nose. In magazines I saw photos of California surfer dudes. They looked really different. They were blonde. They were muscular. Their faces were perfectly proportioned. There were lots of blonde bikini-clad girls hanging around them. I looked at those guys and I thought, "That's what I want to look like. That's what I want to be like." So, when I was eighteen I made my first trip to California. I went to Malibu beach and walked along the water's edge. I saw these same guys that I'd seen in magazines, tanned and buffed. Then it hit me, hard. I realized, *I will never look like that. I will never be like that.* In one crashing moment I understood that *I will never turn into something or someone else. I will always be me.*

I may have had this big realization but I sure wasn't happy about it. My teenage years were mostly pretty miserable, and I had many years after that of feeling bad about myself and struggling. I even felt like I wanted to give up. But I didn't give up and, in the end, what happened? I learned to accept myself and like myself and appreciate what I could offer to the world. I went on to live a life of deepening fulfillment.

You will save yourself a lot of time, energy, and heartache if you learn how to be happy with who you are. Now. No matter how bad you feel at times—and teenage years can plunge you into many a pit of bad feelings—you are not that mess of unhappiness. You are the same person who was once a bright, shining, happy baby, and who can be a happy, fulfilled adult. If that sounds like I'm saying, "Just get through these teenage years," I'm not. I'm saying that the happy baby and eventually happy adult are connected by the teenager: *you*. You can be a miserable teenager or you can be a happy, successful one. You can be engaged and fully alive, *right now*. I'll say it again: you can be happy and you can be successful right now. You don't have to suffer through your teenage years. Your teenage years are the time to begin living, consciously, by choice, into the fullness of who you are.

Happiness—what I'm calling "success"—will be yours as you learn to be more calm, confident, and focused. I know this because I've coached many people like you to live this way and their lives have blossomed.

At this point many teenagers say to me, "Dr. B, you have your head in the clouds. You have no idea how hard my life is!" But I beg you to remember that I was the skinny kid who was so unhappy that he desperately wanted to look like somebody else. Moreover, I wanted to *be* somebody else. I really, really didn't like who I was. I didn't think I was smart, I didn't think I was talented, I didn't think other people liked me, and on and on. Ultimately, the way I learned to like myself was to learn to be calm, confident, and focused. I'm writing this book because I believe you can have a much easier time of life—particularly in your teenage years—than I did.

How to Handle Stress

In this book I'm going to take you through a process. We'll look at how you handle challenges and, particularly, how you handle stress. For instance, if you have a disagreement with someone at home do you become anxious and tense and storm out of the room, or do you know how to stay calm and work it through? If you are facing an important performance—a test, a recital, or an athletic event—do you doubt whether you can handle it, or do you have the confidence that you can perform well? When you have to study for a test do you procrastinate and then cram, or do you focus and study well?

Like everyone else, you have habits in dealing with life's situations— particularly the stressful ones. Rather than labeling your habits "good" or "bad," we'll call them "productive" and "unproductive." Productive habits create happiness and success; unproductive habits create strife and disappointment. We'll look at your habits. What are your productive habits? How can you transform your unproductive habits? And we'll look at all of this in the various situations you face on a daily basis—in school, at home, and in other activities.

At this point you may be thinking, "My life would be OK if it wasn't for_____ [fill in the blank: my sister, my teacher, my friend, my history final, my college applications]. If all that changed, my life would work!" Well, I have news for you, that kind of thinking is *unproductive*. It won't get you anywhere. Why? Because the only person you can really change is yourself.

Perhaps you're thinking, "Actually, my life works pretty well, I don't really need this book." You might be right and I'm glad to hear it. But I still say give it a try. This book will validate what you are already doing and show you how you can do it better.

You may have noticed that the title of this book isn't *Dr. B's Bag of Magic Tricks for Teens*. There's no kit with a top hat and a wand that you wave over your head and then, *Presto!* You can now sail through your life without doing anything. My job as a coach is to show you what to do. Your job is to do it. For some people, that's not an easy thing. It isn't that the information is hard or the message indirect. The material presented here is very direct and clear. The problem is that they don't particularly want to work for a solution to their problem. They want someone else to solve their problems for them. Perhaps they're hoping this book will do it.

Over the years, I have discovered that there are two groups of people: those who are ready to work for change and those who want a quick fix. The latter often come into my office cramped with anxiety or gloomy with depression. After the first session, they are filled with hope and enthusiasm. They come to the second session all pumped up saying, "This is great, I get it." But several weeks later they call or email, moaning in a most painful way, "Oh, Dr. B, I'm still so stressed out! I'm messing up. Everything's going down the tubes! I haven't done any of the exercises you gave me. Do you have any more tips?"

Yes, I do have more "tips," but what good will they do if the person won't follow them anymore than they who worked with my original tips? If you want the results, you have to follow the coaching. Ultimately, you have to become your own coach. There's no way around it. And if you do, the rewards are great. I have watched high school students raise their SAT scores by 200 to 300 points. I've watched teenagers turn around their relationships with their parents and friends. I've seen athletes win games and musicians succeed in auditions. The bottom line is this: people who practice being calm, confident, and focused become their personal best by working through and overcoming challenges.

Be Present

In facing the challenges, they learn life's most important lesson: be present. You know that phrase they use at raffles, "You have to be present to win"? The same is true of life. Only by being present can we develop the awareness that we're veering off track and then get back on track. How many times in your life have you had to admit that you screwed up because you didn't show up?

There is a real correlation between awareness and excellence, but awareness doesn't happen accidentally. Usually, our minds are wandering far from home, leapfrogging from the past into the future, oblivious to what's in front of us. To cultivate awareness and achieve your highest potential, you have to train yourself to bring your awareness to bear on the present moment and to practice being calm, confident, and focused. When you learn how to master yourself you will feel empowered to take these skills into any part of your life. You will have taught yourself to be strong, responsible, and embodied when confronted with a difficult person or a challenging task. You can use that knowledge anywhere you go.

As long as you are willing to do the work to become a success, I can coach you through the process. A good part of this process is you becoming more aware of yourself. In the coming chapters, I will be asking you questions about your thoughts, feelings and experiences. I recommend you use a special notebook or journal to record your answers. Your journal will be a safe, private place for you to go and reflect on what we'll be looking at together.

The Purpose of Your Life

Before we move on, I want to ask you a question: have you ever wondered what the purpose of your life is? Here's what I say: *The purpose of your life is to become the person you are meant to be and to make a positive contribution to the world we share.* Life is about becoming and being your highest self and offering what you can to others to help them along the same path.

When you want a flower to grow in your garden, you go to the nursery and buy a packet of seeds. You can see exactly what you're going to end up with because there is a beautiful color picture of the fully-grown flower on the front of the packet. But when you open it, what do you find? Tiny black lumps that look like mouse droppings. Does that discourage you? No, because you know what these seeds are meant to become. You set up the environment for the seeds to grow. You prepare the soil. You plant the seed and then make sure you give it the right amount of sunlight and water. When that tiny seedling finally sprouts, it is delicate, and you protect it and care for it until it grows into the flower it is meant to be. It takes its place in the garden and is part of a thriving landscape.

I believe that somewhere inside you there is a seed packet with *your* picture on it, a picture of the fully realized you. It's not easy to grow this flower. There are challenges all along the way. But when you face them, you learn from them and you grow with them. Through this process, you grow into the flower in full bloom. Flowers cannot become fully realized unless they push their way up through the soil and share the sun and space with other plants. Our conditions aren't much different. We have to find our way in the world, and all along we face challenges—tests in school, tests of friendship, physical illness, mental troubles, financial reversals, unfulfilled expectations, and loss.

Though we cannot choose most of the challenges we face in life, we can choose how we're going to face them. Are we going to have a bad experience, crumble under the pressure, run away, or avoid challenges altogether? Or are we going to find the strength and inner resources to rise to the challenges and fully *actualize our potential*? That's the term psychologists use for becoming the person you are meant to be—actualize your potential. Facing your teenage years in the right way will give you this opportunity. When you face the challenges before you right now, learn from them and grow with them, you become that person. The challenges in your life require you to call on the inner resources residing deep inside you. By doing that, you come to know yourself and to develop your innate capacities. That is what we mean by actualizing your potential, and being challenged presents you with the opportunities to do it.

Fortunately, we don't have to reinvent the wheel here. There are exquisite role models who have preceded us and can show us how to face the ups and downs of life in a meaningful way. These are the teachers and masters, saints and sages, the divinely inspired women and men who dedicated their lives to finding meaning and purpose through their struggles. Jesus on the cross, Buddha under the Bodhi tree, Moses in the desert, Mohammed in the cave. Each faced the challenges that life handed them, and they mastered the ability to learn and grow and become fully realized beings. We may not all be sages and saints, but we all face challenges on a regular basis, and some of them are severe and daunting. Do we have the strength to overcome, the fortitude to persevere, the humor to see things in a lighter way? With these capacities, it is possible to do more than just get by. We can do something inspiring with our lives. Great beings create a memorable path through life's tests. Because ultimately, that's what life is—a path with tests at every bend in the road. And every test is there to help us grow and to fully become the people we are meant to be.

The word "teenage" covers a seven year span that is momentous, tumultuous, and varied. The experiences of someone about to turn thirteen and still in middle school are vastly different than that of the nineteen-year-old who is on her way to college, or entering the job market, or about to start a family. As you'll soon see, what I am offering are *life* skills and I am trusting that you, the reader, will apply the insights and tools given here at whatever point you are in this span of great growth and transformation called your teenage years. It is your life, after all, and you are moving into the driver's seat.

If you're committed to thinking, "My life sucks and I can't do anything about it," this is probably not the book for you. But even then, I invite you to test out what's in here. Many people I know and have worked with have turned their lives around, just as I did. It's entirely possible for you, too. You can learn to be calm, confident, and focused. Why do I say that? Because the bottom line is this: you are meant to be successful.

If that's what you want, I can coach you.

Let's go for it.

CHAPTER 2

Performance and Stress

Human Performance

I'm a performance coach. People come to work with me when they want to improve their performance. I work with teenagers and surgeons, actors, athletes, executives, and all kinds of people taking tests. I'm often asked, "How can you coach so many different people? How can you help a golfer improve her golf game? Do you play golf? How can you help a student score higher on his AP Biology exam? Do you know all about AP Biology?"

Here's what I answer: "I know about human performance and what everyone needs to perform at his or her best. While I don't know as much as the people who come to work with me—I don't play golf, I never filled a tooth, I haven't run a major corporation, and I haven't taken the AP Biology exam—I know what makes performance successful." Of course, the next question is, "And what is that?"

The answer is simple. The common denominator across every field of human endeavor is the person, and in every field it's the person who has to perform. What I have learned, researched and taught over many years can be applied to anything human beings do. Anyone can improve their performance by learning to be calm, confident, and focused.

You may well ask, "But this is a book about teenagers. What does being a teenager have to do with performance?"

The dictionary defines the word "performance" as the action or process of carrying out or accomplishing an action, task, or function, and I think of performance in this broad way. In other words, no matter what you're doing—whether you're a doctor working with her patients, a basketball player sinking a three-point shot, a pianist playing a recital, a lawyer sitting for the Bar exam, or a teenager in history class—you are performing. Think of your performance as the act of being and becoming yourself. Your parents are performing as parents, your teachers are performing as teachers, and you are performing as a teenager. Successful performance means that your parents, your teachers, and you are accomplishing that task well. You can succeed at being who you are.

The Constant Is You

When people come to me for performance coaching, my first thought is this: What does this person need to perform at his or her best? Of course, they have to learn the subject matter—the sport, the music, the medicine—I never make light of that, but that is only part of the picture. As you know from school, subject matter is always changing. You might have a test in algebra today, a chemistry quiz next week, an oral presentation in history the week after. But there is one thing that doesn't change, one constant at the center of everything you do in life, no matter what the subject, no matter what the setting. That constant is you, the individual. It might be a driving test or a diving test. It may be your relationship with your parent or your relationship with a friend. Whatever the challenge is for you, you are the one who is facing it.

The question you have to ask yourself is this: "What can I learn about myself that will help me perform better in any situation? How can I take control of this process?" Unfortunately, our schools generally do not give students the personal tools they need to help them deal with challenging situations—be they tests in school or in life. Courses and books address only the object of study, not the subject. The common use of the word subject is the material being studied, but in reality, the subject is you.

When I say, "The constant is you," I mean that you are what is certain and continual in all of your life situations. Certainty refers to something that stays the same in spite of outer conditions. Imagine what it would be like to have this certainty in yourself when you face any challenge, the firm faith that you will succeed under any circumstances. On a test in school you might feel rushed, you might be tired, or you might be under extreme pressure to achieve a high score. You might break a pencil or lose your place. During a musical performance you might miss a beat. In an argument with a friend you may suddenly lose confidence in your point of view. Whatever the challenge, whatever the environment, performance coaching can teach you how to be constant in yourself so you can perform at your best.

Stress and Performance

Across the board, in every field of human endeavor, there is one factor that affects performance positively and negatively, and that is *stress*. As I said a moment ago, we teach people all kinds of things in schools and universities—countless subjects in many different fields—but our school systems usually neglect teaching people about stress and how to deal with it. Again, we assume that success means learning the subject matter. But I've seen scores of people who are very knowledgeable and experienced at what they do—whether it's playing the trumpet or being a swimmer—but when it comes time to perform they stress out and lose it. Why is this important? Because when you have to deal with a difficult situation—when you have to perform—the way you feel about yourself and your ability to stay grounded and present largely determines how successful you will be. Understand that the *quality* of the experience in any challenge directly affects the *results*.

The reason for this is simple: stress affects performance. This is well known in many fields, especially in sports. Athletes need a certain amount of stress to charge them up so they can perform at their best. But if the stress crosses a certain line—either too much stress or too little—it starts hurting their ability to do well. This concept is known as the "zone of optimal functioning."

Get in the Zone

The amount of stress needed to produce optimal performance, the amount considered healthful, is different for each person. Some people have to feel extremely worked up to jump-start themselves to perform well. Others will feel jangled and nervous with that much stress, and it will destroy their concentration. For each person there is a zone of optimal functioning where the level of stress is just right. They are stimulated just enough to be creative and energized, to solve problems rationally, and to achieve a sense of self-satisfaction in their performance. Their adrenaline is not pumping too hard nor are they lethargic, so they are able to progress at a good rate.

This book is designed to show you how to find and stay in your zone of optimal functioning as a teenager, whether you're at home, at school, or you're with your friends. By reading the examples and doing the exercises, you will learn how to control stress rather than let it control you. It's unrealistic to think you won't have any stress. But you need to know how to keep your stress at an optimal level so that it charges you up and keeps you at the top of your game rather than letting it wear you out, make you perform sub-optimally, and run you into the ground.

Performing Optimally

The relationship between stress and performance is one of the most thoroughly researched phenomena in the field of psychology. It was first investigated over a hundred years ago, and it look

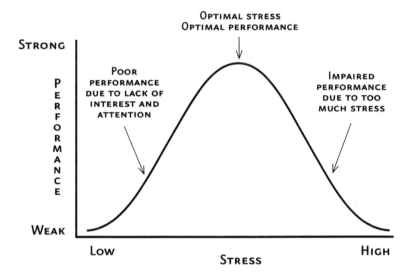

As you can see, when your stress escalates to the point of discomfort, your effectiveness diminishes. When there's too much stress, you leave "the optimal zone." The result is your problem-solving skills contract and your self-esteem and confidence decline. You have trouble staying focused so you feel tense, sometimes to the point of feeling sick or exhausted. At this point, your temper is short, fuses blow, and your performance goes down the tubes.

This relationship between stress and performance holds true whether you are performing in a play, playing a baseball game, delivering a speech, or having a heated discussion with a family member or friend. Again, to most people, a *performance* suggests something that happens on a stage or an athletic field. But if we think of performance as an *action*, an act of carrying out something, performance involves learning how to be fully present in the moment, right there when you have to act. It doesn't matter how well you did something last week, or how well you will do tomorrow; the only thing that counts is how you perform *now*. This state of *performing at your best in the present moment* is well known to athletes, stage performers, surgeons, and many, many others who must bring their knowledge, training, and experience to bear *right now*. I want you, as a teenager, to learn how to do it just like the pros.

Remember, knowing and performing are not the same thing. On a test in school, knowing refers to the comprehension of content. Performing refers to what you *do* with what you know. This is true in any field, and it is true in life. The primary complaint I hear from my clients is that they know what they're supposed to know and do, but when faced with the challenge they get "stressed out" and they can't perform. The bottom line is that to be successful, you have to *deliver* what you know. Often you know what to do; but when you let stress get in the way, carrying it out is another matter. Because stress has a direct impact on your performance, it is essential that you learn how to recognize it and reduce it so that the stress is not destructive. This is the key to your success in anything you do in life. A good part of this book is dedicated to helping you become more aware of your stress before it gets out of hand.

What Is Stress?

When I begin working with my teenage clients, the first question I always ask is, "What do you think causes your stress?" Here are some of the things they tell me:

- "My parents."

- "Too much homework."

- "My little sister."

- "If I don't receive good grades, I won't be accepted by a good college."

- "Teachers. They don't get me."

- "There are too many other things going on in my life."

- "My friends put a lot of pressure on me."

- "Tests make me nervous."

When you hear statements like these, you're probably thinking, *Yep, that just about covers all the bases.* But what if I told you those weren't the bases? What if I said none of those "reasons" are actually the cause of your stress?

We all seem to think that stress comes from other people, too little time, exorbitant expectations, unfavorable comparisons with others, and so on. I know it looks as if these conditions are the source of your stress, but they aren't. These are merely part and parcel of *living*. They include all the conditions of your *life*. Conditions in and of themselves do not cause stress. If they did, everyone who lived under the same conditions would react exactly the same way and succumb to stress. As you'll see, this is not the case. Many people have the ability to successfully manage the conditions.

I can hear you thinking, *But all of those things really* do *cause a lot of tension.* There's no question about it, life is stressful. As you'll see, I have a different theory about what causes stress. It starts with looking at what you are doing when you face something challenging or difficult, be it a test in school, an upset parent, a piano recital, or an angry friend.

Your Reaction Is Stressful

Whether it's difficult siblings, demanding teachers, inconsiderate friends, pushy parents, challenging tests, a boring job, or a high-stakes athletic competition, all of these things are conditions that exist outside of your skin. They are never within your control, and we all know that when the going gets rough, if you had your way, they wouldn't be there at all. These conditions don't really affect you, however, until you let them get under your skin. That's when you transform them from external factors to internal problems.

In any situation you will have a reaction to outside events, and it will either be pleasant, unpleasant, or neutral. That's the range. When your reaction is unpleasant, that's what we call stress because it causes you to reject what's happening. The string of thoughts goes something like this: *I don't like what's going on. Something is wrong. I want this situation to change. I want it to go away.* The first clue that an outside event is causing a stress reaction is that all of a sudden, you cannot relax and you want things to be different. You can't accept this moment just as it is. Whenever something has to change or you won't be happy, that is the experience of stress.

Not everyone has an unpleasant reaction to the same events. Imagine two people taking the same test: Sally is sitting at a desk on the left and Judy at a desk on the right. Sally is sure she is going to fail. Her body is tense, she's doubting herself, and she can't stay on task. Judy, on the other hand, is working through each question, one at a time, in a calm, confident, and focused way.

Many people taking a test will identify with Sally. They are nervous. They exhibit physical symptoms (headache, stomachache, stiff neck), they are attacked by self-doubt, and they can barely keep their mind on the page. The result is they fail or receive poor scores that don't match up with their ability or effort.

Or maybe their scores turn out to be respectable in spite of the strains upon them. But there's hidden damage. They may do well, but they suffer far too much. Taking tests causes them a great deal of anguish and anxiety, yet they still manage to be fairly successful on test after test. They don't do anything about their discomfort because they don't think that it can change. When I ask about the possibility of improving the experience, they shrug their shoulders and say, "That's just the way it is. Tests are a pain in the butt. I hate them, but I do all right." You can substitute any "challenging situation" for "tests."

So there are two categories of people like Sally: either they're miserable and they fail, or they're miserable and they succeed. It's good to succeed, but the process doesn't have to be as insufferable as sitting on a pack of thumbtacks.

Now let's talk about Judy. Those who identify with this individual are not agitated when they face something demanding like a test. Somehow, they are much calmer, they believe in themselves, and they are able to stay on task. The taking of the test, the amount of time they have to take it, and the expectations upon them to do well—*none* of these factors triggers a negative reaction. Their scores are good to excellent without all the drama. In other words, they accept the conditions *as they are* and do what they need to do to manage them well. They don't *feel* stressed.

So here's the important question: what are you doing that causes you to feel so much stress?

The Three Basic Stress Reactions

If you suffer from feeling stressed anywhere in your life you are doing one or more of the following:

- You are holding tension somewhere in your body.

- You are thinking negatively about yourself and how you're doing.

- You are becoming distracted.

Earlier I said that stress is a pressure, strain, or demand. These definitions match up perfectly with the above list. When you grow physically tense, when you think negatively about your performance, or when you are distracted from completing the task at hand, you are putting unnecessary pressure, strain, and demands upon yourself. You know this is happening because you feel like you're being punished or threatened. You may also feel exhausted, uncomfortable, and panicked. The physical tension, the negative thoughts and the distractions—these are all burdens you are placing on yourself, and they negatively impact your performance. In other words, you are making any situation much harder than it has to be.

In the next chapter we'll go into the three stress reactions in more detail and look at how you are disconnecting from yourself in ways that cause you to feel stressed.

CHAPTER 3

Disconnection

Body, Mind, and Spirit

Often, when I'm working with someone like you, one of the first questions she asks is, "Why is being calm, confident, and focused the foundation for success? Why not honest, alert, and funny, or some other combination of three qualities?" It's a good question.

First, you have to understand that you are a whole person, one package made up of three interconnected systems called your body, mind, and spirit. That's your team. When you do anything in life—take a test, do your homework, hang out with friends, play basketball, have dinner with your family—all three team members—your body, mind, and spirit—are there in the room. Like any winning team, if you want to be successful, each team member has to operate at their very best, and all have to cooperate fully. When your body is calm, your mind confident, and your spirit focused, your team will perform at its best.

Disconnecting

The three stress reactions I talked about in the last chapter—physical tension, thinking negatively, and being continually distracted—are the opposite of being calm, confident, and focused. What's more, they have something in common. They all involve pushing away what you need to deal with right now.

I call it *disconnecting*. Since disconnecting is an important concept that threads through this entire book and is an integral part of my performance model, I'm going to tell you what I mean by disconnection and then show you how it actually causes your stress.

First, think about the word *disconnection*. What images come to mind? Here are some that occur to me:

- A telephone line going dead

- Pulling a plug out of a socket

- A head popping off a body

- A wheel flying off a car

The word *disconnect* is made up of two parts. The Latin origin of *dis* means, "separate, move apart, go in different directions." *Connect* means to "fasten or tie together." So to *dis*-connect means to pull apart something that is already together. What is the result? Disruption. Disharmony. Disarray. If you're talking on your cell phone and suddenly you can't hear the other person, the transmission has been disconnected. There is no more communication. If you're reading a book and someone trips over the lamp cord and yanks the plug out of the wall, the light goes out. If you are running the bath water and a pipe outside bursts, the water shuts off. When disconnection takes place out in the world, things cease to function.

This is the same for you. When you disconnect in one of your three "parts"—your body, mind, or your spirit—you are going to feel stressed. The bottom line is this: the stress you are feeling is actually caused by your disconnecting in your body, your mind, or your spirit.

Let's look at each in more detail.

The Body

For your body to operate at its best it needs to be *calm*. The easiest way to define "calm" is by its opposite: not "tense."

Jake is on his high school basketball team. At practice he's a good shooter, but for most games the coach keeps him on the bench. In the last game the coach played him and Jake looked very stiff when he shot or passed the ball. "I don't know what happens when I get out on the court," Jake says. "I'm really tight and I don't shoot or pass well."

While Jake knows he's a good player, he's not succeeding when it counts, during a game. He's "tight," not calm. When you're tight your muscles are tense or twitchy or your breathing is stopped or irregular, and you feel agitated.

The body is meant to be healthy and whole; relaxed muscles and good, steady breathing are essential to that unity. When we disconnect within our bodies it means we are losing touch with what's going on inside of us. It's like you've cut out on yourself. You *feel* stressed out but you are not aware that you feel that way because you're holding your breath or tensing your muscles. In other words, by disconnecting in your body you are splitting up its wholeness and causing disharmony within the entire system. Why is this stressful? Because when you stop your breath or tense your muscles you place your body under a strain. Your brain isn't getting the oxygen it needs to survive. Your heart has to pump harder and you feel a rush of adrenaline. Glucocorticoids, the chemicals your body manufactures when it's in danger, start coursing through you, putting your nervous system into a state of excitement. Your body is having a stress reaction, and whether you are directly conscious of it or not, you feel it. You may feel "nervous" or "anxious" or like you're having a panic attack. You might feel an underlying sense of unease, like something's wrong. These uncomfortable feelings have a physical cause, they originate in the body. A tense body cannot perform at its best in challenging, stressful situations.

In chapter four we will examine how and when you disconnect and become tense, and you'll learn the three tools for calming down.

The Mind

For the mind to operate at its best, it needs to be *confident*. Being confident means believing in yourself. It's opposite is being negative and self-doubting.

> Susan is a B student across the board. While she says she's OK with that, she has the nagging feeling that she could do better, at least in some subjects like math. "I know I could get an A in math," Susan says, "but when it comes time to take a math test I get bombarded with negative thoughts like, 'I won't be able to figure this out,' and 'I'm not smart enough.' I'm sure this gets in the way."

Susan's right. Her mind is sabotaging her with negativity.

Mind is a big word. In general, it means the sum total of our consciousness, what we perceive, what we think, what we believe. One of the things the mind does is talk to itself in the form of thoughts. It does this a lot; all the time, in fact, when we're awake. It's like having a talk-radio station on with no "off" switch. There is a continuous chatter going on inside each one of us, commenting on everything we see, think, and feel. *This is green, that's big. She's funny, he's a jerk. They don't like me. Who cares? I care*, and on and on and on. The commentary also covers what everyone else is doing, but in this book, we're going to concentrate on *how you talk to yourself about yourself.* There is a good reason for this: that is the part of your mind that can either help or hinder you when you are facing any life situation. As one of your team players, your mind is, in a way, either your supporter or your critic. Is it bringing out the best or the worst in you?

Why is this stressful? When you say to yourself, *I'm not good enough and I will never succeed*, you are disconnecting from your inner support system. In math terms, negative means subtracting, making into a minus, taking away from. Negative self-statements are no different. They take away your inner support at the moment you most need it in a challenging situation when your capacities should be at their peak. You are disconnecting from the positive side of your mind; you are being disloyal to yourself. In effect, you're being a traitor to yourself. You're giving up in the heat of battle, pulling away, and jumping ship. What you need at such a time are positive, self-affirming, *connecting* messages but you're getting the opposite.

Negative messages are not the truth; they are distortions, because these kinds of statements tend to be global and blown out of proportion. *I'll never succeed. I can't take tests. I don't have what it takes.* While there's always room for healthy self-criticism, these overly dramatic statements distort the real picture. They suggest that something is wrong with you, that you are defective, a certified loser and you might as well give up, none of which would bear up under the evidence (you got this far, didn't you?). Distortion is one way that we disconnect in our minds. We make grossly negative self-statements, we imagine the worst, and then, of course, we want to bolt.

When you feed yourself negative messages, your mind is working against you instead of helping you. You're under all this pressure to perform with no help from this important system. Your mind is sending out a stream of negative statements and pictures: you see yourself failing the test; you hear your parents yelling at you or standing there with looks of profound disappointment on their faces; you imagine all of your classmates passing with flying colors and going on to illustrious careers while you're left behind. You see your teachers feeling very frustrated. What are most people afraid of when they're chastising themselves in this way? They're afraid of looking stupid. They want to avoid this at all costs.

When this negative mental process snowballs, it almost guarantees a poor performance, which means that you probably *will* fail. And this, in turn, sets you up for failing again—a truly vicious cycle.

In chapter five, I will describe in detail how your mind disconnects and becomes embroiled in this dynamic, and I will give you the tools to correct it.

The Spirit

For your spirit to operate at its best, it needs to be *focused*. "Spirit" is a loaded, often misunderstood word. Depending on your experience it could have negative connotations like being required to attend weekly religious services, or heavy moralizing about what is "good" and "bad." As a performance psychologist, I think of spirit in a different way. In this book, I am speaking about spirit as the part that directs us to become what we're meant to be in life. To me it is the highest self, a person's heart and soul. It's the part that moves me to become a psychologist, my wife a novelist, my college roommate a minister, my next-door neighbor a devoted mother.

Spirit defines and drives us to pursue our authentic goals and it supports us in taking actions that are consistent with those goals. Simply put, when you are connected in your spirit, then your actions lead you to your goals. When you are disconnected in spirit, you either don't have goals that are important to you, or your actions lead you away from them. A disconnection from the spirit causes people to be distracted.

> LeShauna knows that she's got what it takes to be a concert pianist. She's been taking piano lessons since she was a little girl, and now, at age fifteen, her teachers and professional pianists confirm her talent and her possibilities. She has the chance at a full scholarship at a major conservatory. But instead of practicing as much as she needs to in order to advance her skills, LeShauna ends up hanging out with friends online or texting them. "I know I should be practicing," she says, "but . . . ." and her voice trails off. Come audition time, she's nervous and messes up several times during the piece.

LeShauna's spirit is telling her what she needs to do ("I know I should be practicing"), but LeShauna doesn't listen to her spirit and disconnects from it. The result: a poor performance.

Spirit is your driving force. Pay attention and follow through on the direction your spirit is giving you and you're well on your way to being successful.

Disconnect from it and you get distraction, confusion, disappointment, sub-par performance, and sometimes failure. This is true in every area of life—not just for people who perform on stage or on the athletic field. Your spirit is always directing you to do what's best—in relationships, in schoolwork, in what keeps you healthy—in short, in every area of your life. When you follow the direction of your spirit you are *focused*.

In chapter six we'll examine your connection to spirit. Are you pursuing goals that are yours or someone else's? Are you staying on track or becoming distracted? Are you staying focused or are you disconnecting?

When You're Feeling Stressed, You're Disconnecting

Your body, mind, and spirit are your personal team. If any one of them is absent or weak you can't maximize your full potential. But if they work together, each operating at top capacity, you'll hit home runs. Every member of your team must fully participate when you face any challenging situation for you to be in your optimal zone. Any disconnection seriously undermines the whole team's efforts.

Remember this: disconnection in your body, mind, or spirit is the real cause of your stress. If you feel anxious, self-doubtful, or distracted, you are disconnecting in ways that are making you feel that way. The flip side of this is that you can start acting in ways to make yourself feel calm, confident, and focused. This takes two things: (1) become aware that you are disconnecting; and (2) use specific tools to reconnect. The sooner you become aware that you're disconnecting and the sooner you use the tools to reconnect, the better. Then stress won't have a chance to build, and your performance, in every area of your life, will stay steady.

In the next chapter we'll look at where you disconnect and we'll assess where you need to put more attention so you don't feel so stressed. Is it your body? mind? spirit? or some combination of all three?

But before that, we're going to have a reality check.

Let's take a short pause between chapters. I've given you a lot of information so far, and I've hit you with two big, heavy concepts: (1) that whatever the conditions of your life, you are making your life more stressful by how you react; and (2) if you want to make your life more successful, you need to make some changes in how you act. This is the foundation of this book and how I coach people.

I'm calling this little section a "Reality Check" because, if you're like most teenagers, the reality is that sometimes your life sucks. Believe me. I know that from working with people like you and from my own life. As I told you at the beginning, my teenage years were often miserable.

Let's be clear: *life is hard* and your teenage years can be *really hard*.

When you're a teenager, you sometimes feel like you're being flooded by a tsunami of feelings. On any one day you can feel good, bad, anxious, peaceful, alert, dull, focused, distracted, confident, self-doubtful, calm, tense, sociable, isolating, horny, don't-touch-me (what's the opposite of "horny"?), smart, stupid, critical, accepting, resistant, compliant, engaged, and aloof. Sometimes you can have many of these conflicting feelings in one hour. And I'm sure that list just scratches the surface.

Plus, you may feel that people in your life are loving, hurtful, kind, mean, appreciative, resentful, supportive, competitive, and cynical. You may also feel that those who say they understand really do not.

Overall, if we were meeting in person you might shout at me, "YOU DON'T GET IT, DR. B. I'M STRESSED OUT." So let's establish this right now: I *do* get it. I coach people like you on a daily basis. And I was that way, too. In fact, I was so that way that patterns set up in my teenage years grew and spiraled out of control for years to come. As a young adult I was anxious, filled with resentment, and I abused drugs. And then it took years to get out of *that* mess. So I do know what I'm talking about. While I or anyone else cannot save you from whatever you're going through or will go through in your life, I can tell you this: whatever is going on with you, no matter how bad it is, you can turn it around.

Know this: there is a big difference between action and reaction. If you feel your life sucks, a big reason for it is that chances are you are living in a reactive mode. The conditions around you (the people, the situations, the circumstances) are terrible, and you are reacting to them by complaining, shutting down, medicating yourself, or running away. I want to strongly encourage you, while you are reading this book, to believe that you can live your life in an *active* mode. You can take charge of yourself. You just need to know how to do it. That's what this book is all about. That's what people who live happy, fulfilled lives do. They take charge of their bodies, their minds, their spirits, and they do what will make them calm, confident, and focused.

If you want to make some changes in your life then continue reading. If you don't, then either hold onto this book until you do, or give the book away to someone who does. Don't waste your time and energy resisting. This is not about me, the coach, being right. I didn't make up the tools—they come from the best teachers and the most extensive research available in psychology, physiology, and spirituality. What I did was put it all together in one system so you can benefit from this wisdom now and not have to watch your life unravel and fall apart and *then* learn all this stuff. You can learn from other people's experiences as well as your own. The tools to live an easier, more successful life are available to you *now*. If you want them, keep reading.

One more point here. Teenage years are a lot about establishing your independence from your parents. They may want one thing for you while you want something else. In my professional experience, and with rare exception, parents want the best for their kids. How they put that across to them, however, is quite another matter. Their good intentions sometimes end up as screaming matches. The process of parent-child separation can be difficult and messy. Not just for you, but for them, too. Many parents have their own issues of control and with letting go. If you have a difficult relationship with your parents, you may well start to develop a different attitude toward them as you work through this book. I'm not guaranteeing it, since it takes a commitment on their part, too.

After reading this far, you might think, "That's what my mom says!" or "That's what my dad tells me all the time." While that may be true, because truth is truth, I'm not your parent. I'm your coach. I'm telling you all this stuff because I know this can make you a winner in *your* life.

And, just so you know, at the end of this book there's a chapter for your parents which I'll want you to give to them.

Chapter 4

The Three-legged Stool

Your body, mind, and spirit form a natural triad, and a triad is a powerful figure. It's the fundamental structure of harmony in music. In geometry, a three-legged configuration is the sturdiest of structures, much more stable than one that is four-legged. The three-pointed figure always stays a triangle, unlike a square that can be pushed into a parallelogram, or a circle that can be squished into an oval. This unity of three is a potent structure. It shows up in religious traditions and symbols, and it comprises the totality of who you are: body, mind, and spirit.

When I work with clients, I hold up a three-legged stool when I introduce them to the idea that to improve their performance they need a calm body, a confident mind, and a focused spirit.

The three-legged stool, a structure that is ages old, is one of the sturdiest, most durable, and long-lasting constructions ever produced. In the past, people used it for milking cows and sitting around fireplaces. This structure forms a three-point foundation that resists toppling. Visualize one, and then imagine that each leg represents a different part of you. One leg is your body, one is your mind, and the third is your spirit. All three together make up the totality of who you are. They are all part of the same unified structure called "you."

Each leg also represents what's necessary to succeed.

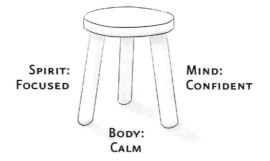

SPIRIT:
FOCUSED

MIND:
CONFIDENT

BODY:
CALM

When all three legs of the stool are equally strong, it is remarkably robust, so strong, in fact, that a baby elephant can rest its full weight on it. When your body, mind, and spirit are sturdy and stable, you have a powerful platform on which to build your own optimal performance in whatever you do in life. All your parts—your team members—are contributing to the integrity and potentiality of the whole.

Life is full of unavoidable challenges, and you need a strong foundation to meet them successfully. If you were taking a trip across the ocean, you would want a ship that would stand up to a storm. If you are going camping, you want a tent that will stand up to the wind and rain. When you're taking a test, you want be sure you can depend on your own internal structure to withstand the challenge of difficult questions. You need to trust that your "inner team" will be dependable in the face of anything the test throws at you. A strong foundation of body, mind, and spirit makes up your three-legged stool—a platform that will support you.

But what happens if one of the legs is weak or short? The stool wobbles and loses its stability. Any leg that is weak imposes a strain on the entire system, which places excess pressure on the other two. What happens if that baby elephant tries to stand on a stool with one fragile leg? The whole thing collapses and the elephant falls on its rear end. You operate the same way. You need each leg of your stool to do its job and for all three to be equally strong. If one leg is weak, it will pull the other two down with it.

What does your three-legged stool look like? I have designed a self-diagnostic tool to help you take a snapshot of yours. The Bernstein Performance Inventory (BPI) will give you a reading on which of your legs is the weakest and which is the strongest in challenging and stressful situations. The BPI is made up of nine questions and takes five minutes to complete. By diagnosing yourself, you will find out which leg has been holding you back. You'll identify what your problem area is and where to apply your attention.

The Bernstein Performance Inventory (BPI)

Recall a recent situation in which you had to face a challenging or stressful situation in a particular time and place. It can include taking an examination, having a conflict with a friend, learning to ski in front of an instructor, talking with a parent, or singing before an audience for the first time.

Visualize the details of the event, remembering the situation as clearly as you can. What happened and how did you feel about it? In a few words, describe in your journal what the performance context was (SAT, GRE, musical audition, athletic competition, etc.) and how you felt about it.

Below are nine statements. Read each one and record in your journal the appropriate number to the right of the statement to indicate how you felt during this performance situation.

Before the Situation Began:

How I Felt	Not at All	A Little Bit	Some-what	A Lot
1. I felt calm and relaxed.	0	1	2	3
2. I was confident in my abilities.	0	1	2	3
3. I was able to focus on the task and do what I needed to do.	0	1	2	3

As the Situation Proceeded:

How I Felt	Not at All	A Little Bit	Some-what	A Lot
4. I stayed calm the whole time.	0	1	2	3
5. I remained confident for the duration.	0	1	2	3
6. I retained my focus all the way through.	0	1	2	3
7. If I started feeling nervous, I knew how to calm down.	0	1	2	3
8. If my confidence slipped, I was able to retrieve it.	0	1	2	3
9. If I lost my focus, I knew how to get back on track.	0	1	2	3

Scoring Your BPI

To determine your overall scores, total up your answers as follows:

After you have added your scores, make a diagram in your journal like the one below and fill in your total scores (see example below).

CALM
Total your answers for questions 1, 4, 7

CONFIDENCE
Total your answers for questions 2, 5, 8

FOCUS
Total your answers for questions 3, 6, 9

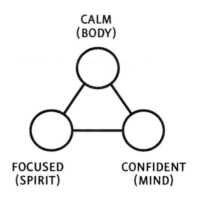

How to Interpret Your Results

As you can see, the above diagram looks like a three-legged stool. Examining the numbers in each of the three circles will tell you what your relative strengths and weaknesses are. Since the highest score you can achieve in any one "leg" is nine, any number less than nine shows that you need to reinforce that leg.

To show you how scores are interpreted and where you can go from there, let me walk you through the example of one of the students I'm coaching.

Sam is a high school senior who is under-performing on his AP History test. His BPI scores: Calm, 2; Confident, 4; Focused, 7.

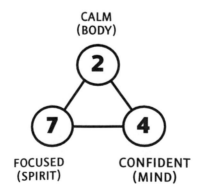

What do these numbers tell us about Sam? Obviously, his strongest leg is Focus, his weakest is Calm, and Confident is somewhere in between. After listening to Sam tell his own story about how he approaches history tests, his BPI scores will make sense to you.

> I might not be a genius, but in general I'm a pretty good student. I mean, I keep on top of my studies and I'm not a slacker. I do all my assignments and turn them in on time, which is a lot more than I can say for most of my classmates. Also, when it's exam time, I don't wait and cram just before the deadline. But unlike all the other tests I have to take, before history tests, and sometimes right in the middle of them, I just get these scary thoughts like, You're totally not capable of dealing with this. There's just too much stuff. Thoughts like these bug me, but they don't really waylay me from doing the job. I can kind of ignore them. What does get in the way is that I feel really nervous. My heart starts pounding, my legs and arms feel weak, and my stomach is in knots. Sometimes I even feel like I can't breathe. These physical symptoms I can't ignore. They usually start right before the test, and on a bad day, they stay that way through the whole hour. When it's really intense, I can barely think.

Sam's score on Focus was 7 out of a possible 9. That's to be expected since he reported that he did all his assignments and kept up a decent study schedule. That means he was connected to his spirit, his driving force, and had no trouble staying on track. Sam's Confidence score, at 4, was shakier. He was, from time to time, beset by negative thinking that undermined his belief in his abilities. Somehow he managed to shake those thoughts off and retain his self-assurance. But Sam was never able to conquer a pure case of nerves. His inability to stay calm in the face of an impending test was his weakest leg. His score of 2 in the Calm leg attests to his difficulties. By his own words we can tell that he was dissociating from his body, which caused him to become more and more physically tense, which in turn made him feel ungrounded. Naturally, the fact that Sam's heart was pounding and he had trouble breathing became a significant distraction. It made it harder to keep connecting to the task at hand. This, in turn, affected his confidence. As his confidence level slipped, he found it harder to rebound. What we can see from this example is how the weakness in this one leg—Calm—put a strain on the entire structure and kept Sam from achieving the grade he should have gotten, considering how hard he studied.

Sam's strongest leg was his ability to stay focused on a goal, so I gave him a new goal to focus on: to learn to become calm in the face of a history test. In no time at all, he learned the three tools for calming down. As the physical tension began to dissolve, we noticed that Sam's ability to focus grew even stronger than it had been before. Naturally, this gave his confidence a huge boost because he had been able to conquer this beast that had caused so much agitation and strain. He grew ever more sure of himself as he was able to remember the material and think through test questions without physical tension overwhelming him.

Remember: working on any one of the legs immediately links you to the other two and makes your whole system stronger.

Your Scores Give You a Starting Point

What does your three-legged stool look like? Which is your strongest leg? Which is your weakest? Recognize that you are not comparing yourself to another person—just to yourself. These scores tell you what *you* need to strengthen in order to reduce your test stress and improve your performance.

As you do this you may be thinking, Hey, wait a minute, Dr. B! My BPI scores aren't accurate. They say that I'm not very confident. But that's not true! I'm usually very sure of myself.

The BPI is not a definitive statement on how you are in every aspect of your life. It is meant to help you examine how you handle challenges and perform under pressure. Take a few moments to consider whether your BPI scores accurately represent how you are in most test situations. Sometimes when people take the BPI, the situation that comes to mind is some horror story about a stressful situation that isn't really typical of their usual performance. Consequently, their BPI scores aren't representative of how they react to most stressful situations. Look at your scores and ask yourself if they are a reflection of how you perform most of the time in stressful situations. If you find that your BPI scores don't reflect your overall performance, then re-take the inventory based on what you are usually like in stressful situations to obtain a more accurate general reading.

Before we go on, look at your scores again. What do you most need to strengthen? Being calm? Remaining confident? Or staying focused?

In the next three chapters, we will take on each leg of the stool. You can begin by working on your shortest leg (your weakest score), by going straight to the chapter that covers it. But you can also start with your strongest score since some people benefit the most by working from their strength. While I recommend that you read sequentially through the next three chapters, this model is not a rigid structure that you have to squeeze yourself into. Its beauty is that wherever you begin, you will end up encompassing the whole. Even if you scored high in one particular leg, it's still important to check out the tools in that chapter because you can always grow stronger. If you happened to score low on all three, that is only showing you that you have room to grow in all three areas.

The end goal of the next three chapters is to teach you to become calm, confident, and focused as you go through your life, facing all the many challenges you have to face, whether it's a test in school, a close relationship with a friend or family member, or anything else you have to deal with that becomes stressful. When you know how to become calm, confident, and focused you will always have a sturdy, stable platform and be ready to perform at your best and be a success at being yourself.

It's All About Staying Connected

I'll sum up this chapter by saying this: if you want to succeed you have to stay connected in your body, mind, and spirit. Since being disconnected means being separated from the whole, being disconnected inside of you means that the body, mind, and spirit are detached from one another. It can also mean that there is a disconnection within any one or more of the three systems.

To put it more simply, when you are faced with a challenging situation—a relationship, a test, a performance—maybe you tense up. Maybe you become afraid and tell yourself you can't handle it. Maybe you find it impossible to keep your mind on the material. You want to escape, to run away. This is disconnecting. It has a purpose. It is a way of coping with a difficult situation. You want to get out of there!

But remember what I said in the first chapter: You have to be present to win. Wishing things were different, avoiding the situation, or "checking out," will not lead to success. In any difficult or challenging situation, when you disconnect, you are pulling away. I don't want to be here. I'd rather be any place but here. The problem is that you have to be there with most situations in life if you want to accomplish your goals, goals that are important and will make a valuable contribution to your life and to the lives of those around you. Sure, you can bail and run away, but that only postpones the inevitable. At some time you're going to have to face whatever difficult situation you are avoiding, like a test in school. Since you cannot not take a test, you may as well stop fighting it and be there. Really be there. By continually trying to run away you are making the whole experience odious and repellent. The test—whether it's in school or in another part of your life—isn't going to go away. Disconnecting from yourself in a vain attempt to disappear in spirit, even if you can't physically remove yourself, doesn't work. The more you disconnect, the higher your stress will be. You're going to feel worse and worse, and your performance in any area of your life will suffer.

In the next three chapters I'm going to give you the tools to stay connected in each member of your "team"—your body, mind, and spirit. You'll be happy to know that there are only nine tools, three for each team member. The tools are simple, intuitive and have been around for hundreds, if not thousands, of years. Human beings have always been on a quest to be more calm, confident, and focused. And those who use the tools succeed. Just as you will.

Before moving on, let's prepare for what's coming. In the next three chapters I'm going to give you exactly what you need to be calm, confident, and focused. You will receive the nine tools necessary for success, at whatever you're doing. These chapters are the heart of this book and of my work.

"Why," you may ask, "is this a 'Reality Check'?"

In the first chapter I said that giving you the tools is necessary, but it is not sufficient for you to be successful. If I offered you something tasty to eat that required a knife and fork and you never picked up the knife and fork, the food would just sit there. You'd never enjoy its pleasurable and nutritional benefits. If the doctor gave you a prescription to cure your flu, and you taped the prescription to your bathroom mirror and never took it to the pharmacist, or if the pharmacist filled the prescription but you never took the medication, nothing would happen. *No change.* That's how it is with the tools I am going to give you. They will sit on the page, like the knife and fork on the table, or the prescription taped to the mirror, until you do something with them.

That's the reality. Unless you're actively involved in the process of using what's in this book, things in your life will stay same old, same old. You have to take what I'm offering and not just think about it—an important first step— you have to use it. I can tell you, from many years of experience, that this is hard for most people. Why? Because we generally prefer to hang out on the couch and hit the remote rather than get up and take action. What's more, in this process you have to be willing to look at yourself clearly and honestly, which also is a real challenge for most people. Unless *you* want to make some changes in how you think and act, and unless you actually make those changes, everything will stay the same

What kind of "changes"? Simply put, we're going to look at your habits and evaluate which ones are productive and which ones are unproductive. Then you're going to do what's necessary to move the unproductive ones into the productive column.

Conventionally we talk about "good habits" and "bad habits." I'm not in favor of this distinction because it has a moralistic tone and suggests someone sitting in judgment deciding what's "good" and what's "bad." I prefer to think of habits as "productive" or "unproductive". A productive habit is an action or series of actions that leads to growth. A productive habit creates success and it doesn't hurt you or anyone else. In fact, it has potential benefits for you and others. On the other hand, an unproductive habit doesn't lead anywhere. Rather than build or grow, an unproductive habit keeps you stuck. It may be harmful to you or someone else.

Given our definition of stress as a function of disconnection, and that disconnection leads to poor performance, we are looking to build productive habits, habits that keep you connected, habits that build a better you and a better environment.

Back to the seed packet analogy: a productive habit would be one that tends the plant and helps it grow so that it can eventually blossom and flower. The productive habit would look like this: watering the garden, weeding it, fertilizing it, and being patient. An unproductive habit would be attending to the plant haphazardly or neglecting it entirely, thinking someone else will take care of it.

Productive habits are ones that connect; unproductive habits disconnect. A productive habit produces a positive result; an unproductive habit produces a negative result. In terms of our model of the three-legged stool, productive habits keep you calm, confident, and focused. Productive habits keep stress at an optimal level. Unproductive habits produce more stress. Your unproductive habits keep you anxious, self-doubting, and distracted. They keep you stressed out.

We are creatures of habit. All of us. Our lives are shaped by our habits: habits of action (walking, talking, eating); habits of thinking (things we like, things we don't like); and habits of feeling (what makes us happy, sad, or angry). Habits are a series of learned actions which we repeat in sequence. We need habits because without them, any action we perform would be as if for the first time. Take the habit of walking into a darkened room and turning on a light. When you cross the threshold into a dark room you are in the habit of reaching to your right for a light switch. Then, you're in the habit of flipping it on. Imagine if you didn't have that habit. Every time you walked into a darkened room you wouldn't know what to do. You'd stay in the dark. Habits provide patterns and give structure to our lives. They also have a lot to do with how well or poorly we handle stress and how well or poorly we perform, which I'll discuss shortly.

In the next three chapters I'm going to give you the specific tools to be calm, confident, and focused. The tools—and there are only nine of them—are the building blocks of all productive habits. Remember, your personal team has three members: your body, mind, and spirit. Each one can have productive or unproductive habits. Ultimately, it's your choice which habits *you* want to cultivate.

One of the great trials of adolescence—of being a teenager—is that you want people to treat you like an adult. But many teenagers keep acting like children. They won't let go of unproductive habits. So why should people treat them like adults? What I'm going to lay out for you in the next chapters gives you the pathway to becoming a responsible adult. When you practice what's here, you are announcing to the world that you deserve to be treated with respect.

If you're rolling your eyes, thinking, *Dr. B, don't tell me that all adults have productive habits. They don't.* I totally agree with you. I know that because I learned it the hard way. I carried my unproductive teenage habits into my 20s and 30s and then had a big mess to clean up. The moral of that story is that if you start cultivating productive habits now, you'll have a much easier time of it as you cross the threshold into the rest of your life. You'll know how to turn on the light and dispel the darkness.

CHAPTER 5

How to Calm Down

Last September, a bright high school senior named Jamal came to see me. Anxiously, he wanted me to help him raise his SAT scores by 200 points so the college of his choice would accept him. He had one last chance to take the test. After that, he was at the mercy of whichever college would take him. Why had he performed poorly?

"Because on the last SAT test," Jamal told me, "I grew more and more nervous as the time went on. I couldn't remember the information I studied, so I started thinking, What hope is there? After I scraped by on three questions in a row, I hit a wall. I just froze up."

As Jamal spoke, his right leg bounced up and down rapidly, his shoulders tensed and rose almost to his ears, and his speech accelerated like a car with a jammed gas pedal. Several times while he spoke, he held his breath. "Just talking about the test makes me nervous," he said anxiously, a comment which of course was unnecessary since his whole body communicated it. "I feel like I'm flipping out right now. This is what happened to me on the SAT."

It was a natural mistake: Jamal believed that remembering the test was making him nervous. In fact, all the nervous things he was doing with his body were causing his anxiety: bouncing his legs, tensing his shoulders, and holding his breath. His body made his mind nervous, not his memories. When I told him this he looked at me like I was from another planet. "My brain is taking the test," he shot back, "not my body. I always sit like this. What does all that have to do with my SAT scores?"

This is a very common misconception. Most people think that only their mind is working on an exam. That's where the information is stored, right?

Not quite.

Since your body is one of the three key players on your team, all of your body is in the room and engaged when you have to perform. If you want to perform at your best, then all of you, not just your brain, has to be fully present and supporting the process. This is as true when you have to perform in any challenging situation, whether it's a test, a ball game, a stage performance, or a difficult interpersonal situation.

Here's an example. Suzanne, a tenth grader, came into my office and said, "My mother is driving me nuts!" "Tell me what you mean," I said. "But close your eyes, imagining the whole scene and tell it to me like you're narrating it." Suzanne looked at me like I was nuts, but she complied and closed her eyes. "As soon as I get home from being with my friends my mom sits me down and asks me a million questions about who I was with and what we did. She doesn't trust me at all. I can't stand it!" As Suzanne spoke there was a whole other scenario going on with her body that I observed and of which she was unaware. Her shoulders tensed up, her brow became deeply furrowed, and her hands clenched tightly. "I get so aggravated!" she said, nearly screaming. I asked her to freeze and open her eyes and look at what was going on with her body. Did she think that her difficulties with her mom had anything to do with how much tension she was adding to the scene? "No!" Suzanne said. "My mother is making me tense."

Sure, from Suzanne's point of view her mom was being a pain in the butt. Suzanne didn't like the feeling of being distrusted. But Mom didn't cause Suzanne's tension, Suzanne did.

Tensing during any challenging situation causes stress. Adrenaline surges through your gut, your blood pressure shoots up, and your entire system goes on alert. Your brain screams *Danger!*—as if a tiger is chasing you. A torrent of stress hormones are unleashed into your bloodstream. It becomes increasingly hard to focus and think. Looking at the test questions or facing your mother's questions can make you want to fight, flee, or panic It looks as if those questions are causing your tension, but questions are just printed words on paper or words coming out of someone's mouth. They aren't doing anything to you. Your stress is mounting and your performance is suffering because you are disconnecting from your own body. You are not aware of what your body is doing, but it's spinning out of control. You may even feel like you want to flee, but you can't. You have to sit there and force yourself to answer the questions.

How can you possibly perform well in the face of all that tension, when you want to run away but can't? These are all forms of disconnection. Remember: disconnection causes stress and too much stress causes poor performance.

It's the same for any type of performance. If a soccer player is sitting on the bench waiting to go into the game and she keeps tensing her body, when the coach finally sends her out on the field she will be nervous right from the start. She'll miss shots she ought to be making and she'll be out of sync with her teammates. It doesn't matter how hard she practiced. She needs to stay loose on and off the field. If a pianist's fingers lock in the middle of a piece, they can't float effortlessly over the keys. Again, it doesn't matter how well he knows the music.

In all these cases, the people disconnected from their bodies. Remember the three-legged stool? Disconnection in one leg immediately hobbles the other two. When you lose the feeling of calm in your body, it precipitates negative thoughts (in your mind) and you'll easily become distracted and lose heart (in your spirit). Stress can build very rapidly and when it grows past a certain point, your performance will suffer. Guaranteed.

To improve your performance in every area of your life you have to learn to reduce the stress in your body. Simply put, when you have to do anything, whether it's taking a test, or dealing with your unruly little brother, you want your body to be calm. I realize that "calm" and "teenager" might seem like a contradiction in terms, In your teenage years you are often filled with lots of energy, sometimes you can hardly sit it feels like so much is going on inside and outside of you. While all that is true, learning how to calm yourself down is a necessary and invaluable skill if you want o be more successful in every area of your life. The rest of this chapter will show you how to do that.

Awareness First

To get your body into a calmer state you need to learn two things:

1. How to recognize when you are *not* calm; and

2. How to use specific tools to calm yourself down.

In this section we'll work on your awareness of your body. We'll pay attention to how your body feels when you are anxiously anticipating a stressful event, or when you are midway through the event itself.

If you're like most people, you are not too aware of your body throughout the day, unless you're in pain or you feel sick. A sore throat, a stomachache, a cold, a fever, and a tooth ache call attention to themselves. But until the discomfort reaches an uncomfortable level, we tend to minimize or even ignore the early signs. It's nothing. It will go away. We don't become aware until the pain is virtually shouting at us. My tooth is killing me! That's when we do something about it.

For certain people this doesn't hold true—people who use their bodies all the time—like dancers, swimmers, or singers. They have to pay close attention and not ignore any signs that all is not well, and then attend to them because their jobs depend on it, often in front of a crowd. The upside is that they are connected to what goes on in their bodies. Most of us don't have that threat hanging over us. The problem we have is that when we ignore the signs of disconnection, it causes stress to build. But ultimately, we face the same failure. It behooves us to increase our body awareness—when we are not calm—so we know how to deal with it at critical times.

Let's start with this question: what signs and symptoms in your body tell you that you are not calm?

I know when I'm not calm because . . .
(*Which apply to you?*)

- My chest feels tight.

- I have a headache or feel one coming on.

- My shoulders ache.

- My neck feels stiff.

- I stop breathing.

- My stomach hurts.

- My heart beats rapidly.

- My muscles ache.

- I start sweating.

- My skin feels prickly.

- I feel tense all over.

- I feel like I'm gasping for air.

- My feet curl up.

- My legs cramp.

- I make fists with my hands.

- I feel like I want to run away.

- My mind starts racing.

- I start talking too fast.

- I bite my nails.

- My nerves are jittery.

- My eyes ache.

- My voice rises.

- I feel generally uncomfortable.

Perhaps you identified with one, perhaps ten. Everyone is different, so consider what other symptoms may be true for you.

People often ask me, "But why is it necessary to be aware first?" Think about it this way. When you are driving a car and you see a sign that says STOP, it is telling you exactly what you need to do: put your foot on the brake and stop the car. If you disregard the sign and keep going, you are risking your own life and that of others. The physical signs of tension in your body are like a stop sign sending you a message. It is your body's way of signaling you that you are disconnected, which is useful to know because it tells you that you need to reconnect to your body and calm down. If you don't pay attention to these signs, you are going to crash.

Awareness of when you are not calm is the first step in the process of reconnecting with your body.

Refining Your Awareness

It doesn't matter how many or how few items you checked above. Becoming aware of what is going on with your body when you are not calm is a big step in the right direction. Besides, there are only three basic ways we human beings lose our sense of calm. Each of your responses, on the checklist, is related to one of these:

1. We stop breathing or we breathe irregularly.

2. We become ungrounded.

3. We shut down in one or more of our five senses.

Before moving on to the three tools for calming down, I would like you to cultivate your awareness of how and when you disconnect from your body. Does something go awry with your breath? Do you lose touch with the floor under you? Do your muscles get tense? Do you stop seeing (or hearing) clearly?

Read through the chart below and think about the questions it is asking you, then answer what you can. If you can't answer all of the questions right now that's fine. You might need to do some observation first so you can collect what us psychologists call "baseline data" on yourself with your journal.

Remember, the more you cultivate your awareness of the ways in which you disconnect from your body, the more quickly you will be able to catch the stress well before it builds. In other words, you will reconnect right away and actually *reduce* the stress. It won't have a chance to reach the point of having a negative impact on your performance. Even better, it will be at just the right level (remember the stress/performance curve on page 14?) so that you can perform at your best.

As you consider the chart, remember a test you recently took or imagine one you are about to take.

Awareness Inventory: Body

When I am in a situation that I feel is stressful, I notice the following things in my body.

In each category, which apply to you?

BREATHING	I hold my breath. My breathing becomes very shallow. I breathe erratically (I gasp, I stop breathing, I take small breaths).
GROUNDING	I'm not aware of the floor or of the chair I'm sitting on. My feet are coming off of the ground. I feel tension in my (name body parts).

SENSING	I tend to close down (i.e. I'm not aware of) these senses:
	
	      Touch Smell Taste
	
	        Sight Hearing

Remember, awareness means paying attention to what's going on inside of you. As you study for a test or take one, you may realize that you are doing all sorts of unhelpful things with your body that you probably didn't notice before. The difference now is that you are going to pay attention and treat the symptoms in your body as road signs to help you stop and reconnect.

The more aware you are, the more effectively you can use the tools I'm about to give you.

The Three Tools for Calming Down

Now you are ready to learn the three tools for calming down. These tools will help you to reduce quickly any stress building up in your body. The tools are easy to learn and effective. If you worked through the last section on awareness you already have a jump start on them.

TOOL #1: Calming Down by Breathing

It should come as no surprise that breathing is the first tool. Let's work on this together.

- Take a good deep breath. Inhale . . . breathe in through your nose.

- Exhale . . . breathe out through your mouth.

- Do it again . . . inhale . . . exhale.

Notice where your breath is going. When I ask people to "take a good deep breath" almost everyone puffs up their lungs and upper chest. This is not a deep breath. A breath that raises your shoulders and expands your chest does not calm you down; it actually amps you up. I call it a "fight or flight breath" because it prepares you to do battle or to run away. This kind of breathing feels like fear. It's what the body does when it's reacting to danger.

Imagine you are walking in a jungle and suddenly a ferocious tiger is facing you, baring its teeth. Fear courses through your body. When you take a big gulp of air while facing a tiger, it goes to your upper chest. Either you're going to face the danger or you're going to run away from it. Either way, this is a survival breath and its purpose is not to relax you.

A calming breath, on the other hand, goes to a different and deeper place—your belly, which is why the first tool is a calming belly breath.

Exercise: The Belly Breath

- To start with, sit comfortably in a chair with your back well supported.

- Place your body in an open position—uncross your arms and your legs. (If your arms or legs are crisscrossed you will restrict your airflow.)

- Rest your palms on your thighs and place both feet on the floor.

- Now place your hands on top of your navel and let your belly just relax. This means don't hold your belly in. (Resist any temptation here to suck in your stomach so you can look thin.) Let your belly hang out and relax. First, exhale through your mouth . . . now breathe in through your nose, but don't suck in your belly. Let it stay expanded. You will feel the breath seep into your lungs as you breathe in, but your chest won't be heaving up and down. Both belly and chest will be calm as your breath keeps dropping down into your lower belly.

- Slowly, breathe in and out three times in this open, expanded position, chest relaxed and belly wide.

- If you want to deepen your breath even more, reach your hands around you and place your palm and fingers on both sides of your lower back right along the hips. Now, breathe deeply down and feel your bottom back ribs very gently expand as you do this. This is a small, subtle movement. You have to be quiet and tuned in to feel it, but as you sense this gentle movement of your ribs you will notice your calmness deepening.

- Now, inhale again, deeply down into your belly and lower back.

- Slowly exhale . . . let the breath out gently.

- Breathe in and out like this three times.

- Feel yourself calming down. Don't force the breath in and out and don't hyperventilate.

At this point you might start yawning or feel sleepy. Many people have this reaction. Recently, a bright, athletic, seventeen-year-old girl came to me for SAT coaching. As she talked about herself she was so charged with energy she could hardly sit still. With lightning speed she rattled off an incredibly long list of activities in which she was involved. I couldn't help but notice that she hardly took a nanosecond to breathe. We started working on deepening and regularizing her breath. In less than five minutes she started yawning. A lot. Then she actually fell asleep! Her system was so tightly wound and deprived of oxygen, so needing to rest, that given the first opportunity to calm down she conked out. So, if you are yawning, are sleepy, or feel light-headed as you start paying attention to and deepening your breath, know that this is actually a good sign. Your body is calming down. It is telling you that it is not used to breathing deeply and regularly, and it needs some rest!

The way to deep belly breathing is to work slowly, gently, and determinedly on cultivating your breath. It may feel a little strange at first and all that oxygen might make you feel a bit light-headed. Your system simply isn't used to taking real breaths. It's used to short, choppy mini-breaths. After a while though, deep, steady breathing will feel like the most natural, calming thing in the world.

Putting Breathing into Action

The next time you notice that you are not calm, treat the anxious feelings like a road sign. If your stomach is churning, or you start sweating, or your legs are shaking, your body is sending you a message: "You need to calm down." This is your awareness kicking in. The first thing to ask yourself is, "How am I breathing?" because it is the most primary question. You've probably stopped breathing or your breathing has become very shallow or irregular. Do the exercise above and you will feel yourself calming down immediately.

Once you have started breathing deeply, regularly say, "Thank you" inside. Why do this? Because the awareness you just received that you were not breathing is a gift. It is a realization to be grateful for. Whether you believe your awareness comes from a God, a Goddess, a Higher Power, your Highest Self, Nature, the Universe, or Life, the very fact that it is coming to you at all is like a present. Gratitude acknowledges the giver and encourages future giving. Imagine receiving a wonderful gift from someone and not saying thank you. The giver wouldn't feel like being generous again, "Well, she didn't say 'Thank you' last time." Expressing gratitude invites more of what you're grateful for to come your way.

What most people do when they notice that they are "breathing wrong" is to beat themselves up—"I can't believe I'm still doing that! When am I gonna learn?" They don't appreciate the awareness at all. This kind of critical response is not allowed! I urge you to try saying "Thank you" every time you become aware of anything that you are trying to change in yourself. Gratitude is the opposite of criticism and it spreads an atmosphere of kindness and compassion—exactly the right atmosphere for inner growth.

Breathing deeply and then saying "Thank you" reduces feelings of stress, and you actually improve the possibility of attaining your goals because you are cultivating a helpful relationship with the powers of change. When you breathe deeply and regularly, you are giving your brain, blood, and body the oxygen it needs to perform optimally. Even if you don't believe in a God, Goddess, or Higher Power, expressing gratitude still cultivates a better relationship with your own consciousness and highest self (the best person you can be).

TOOL #2: Calming Down by Grounding

Mike is about to have a college interview. He is sitting in a room full of other high school seniors. Everyone is fidgeting. You can smell the anxiety in the air. Mike himself is perched on the edge of his chair, one foot coiled around the leg. His other foot is lifting off of the ground, knee and leg bouncing. He is definitely not calm. What is wrong with this picture?

Mike is very ungrounded.

Becoming grounded has two parts. The first part is feeling supported by the floor and the chair. To have this experience, do the following simple exercise as you continue reading:

Exercise: Grounding Yourself

- Start by sitting comfortably, upright, in a chair.

- Uncross your arms and your legs.

- Place your feet flat on the floor.

- Breathe down to your belly.

- Now, feel the floor under your feet.

- Feel the floor supporting your feet.

- Now feel your body sitting on the chair.

- Feel your legs and butt and back touching the chair. If the chair has arm rests, feel your arms being supported by them.

- Feel your whole body being supported by the floor and the chair.

This is the first part of grounding. Continue the exercise for one minute and enjoy the feeling that comes over you.

Did you remember to breathe? Most people, when they start learning how to ground themselves, often stop breathing! Don't let that happen. You can use two tools simultaneously just by keeping your breathing deep and steady as you ground yourself by feeling the support of the floor and chair.

The combination of breathing and grounding is very powerful and goes a long way toward connecting you to your own body, calming yourself down and staying present.

The second part of grounding is letting go of physical tension. Let's look at Susan again, a little further into the test. Now her shoulders are hiked way up and her brow is deeply furrowed. Her left hand is making a fist and her right hand is tightly squeezing the pencil. All of this is physical tension. When you hold tension in your body you are actually pulling away from gravity, which is a great settling force. Gravity draws everything in us to the earth. When you tighten muscles in your legs, neck, back, or forehead, you are pulling away from the earth, ungrounding yourself.

In the awareness section of this chapter you identified the areas in your body where you hold tension. Now, let's use the tool of grounding to release that tension. Another name for grounding is letting go. This means just what it says. Let go of—release—wherever you are holding tension. Let gravity work. Let the tension flow out of you and into the ground. Practice this by tightly clenching an object in your hand. Start with something soft like a small stuffed animal, an old tennis ball, or a bunched up T-shirt. Now clench it really tightly and heighten that tension. Squeeze it even more tightly. Good. Now let go. Relax your hand muscles. The object will drop to the ground. Feel the wave of calm pass through your whole body.

To practice letting go in your body, try an exercise called the "Tension/Release Scan."

Exercise:
Tension/Release Scan

- Sit comfortably in a chair, arms and legs uncrossed.

- Tighten the muscles in your left foot and leg.

- Now, with an exhale, release the leg muscles.

- Tighten the muscles in your right foot and leg.

- With an out-breath, release them.

- Tighten the muscles in your belly.

- Breathe out and release.

- Tighten the muscles in your left hand and arm.

- Breathe out and release.

- Tighten the muscles in your right hand and arm.

- Breathe out and release.

- Tighten your chest and shoulders.

- Breathe out and release.

- Tighten your neck muscles.

- Breathe out and release.

- Tighten your jaw muscles.

- Breathe out and release.

- Tighten your whole face.

- Breathe out and release.

- Tighten your whole body.

- Breathe out and release.

After this exercise, locate the area in your body where you store the most tension. Is it your jaw? Your lower back? Your legs? Wherever it is, feel the tension there, hold it, and even heighten it for five seconds. Now, on an out breath, let it go. Release the tension into the ground. At the same time feel yourself supported by the floor and chair (the first form of grounding). Doing this expertly sets you well on the way to calming down. That phrase has more meaning now, doesn't it?

TOOL #3: Sensing

The third tool for calming yourself is sensing. It is easy to turn on one of your five senses—seeing, hearing, touching, tasting, or smelling—when you become aware that you are anxious. As you make the connection through your senses to the world around you, you will start feeling more calm in your body.

What is the relationship between opening your senses and calming down? This tool is a little more complicated than the first two, so stay with my explanation below and you will reap great rewards.

Your senses connect you to the world. They tell you what you are looking at, listening to, tasting, touching, or smelling. Without your senses you wouldn't know where you were or what was happening around you. You would feel very disconnected, which would be frightening. A well-known psychology experiment proved this. When people were placed in a pitch-black, soundproof room they immediately became disoriented. Soon they grew severely anxious. Why? They had no reference points to anything familiar. They were cut-off and adrift, disconnected from any sensory input. Sensory input is connection, how we make contact with our world. Since stress is a function of disconnection, it makes logical and practical sense that to reduce stress, anxiety, and tension, you want to increase your connection, this time, through your senses.

Let's start with your sense of sight. Optometrists notice that when we are anxious, our sight tends to be compromised, as is reflected in the phrase, "He has tunnel vision." Commonly, we use the phrase to describe a person who is not taking in the whole picture. We might say, "John, who believes that high school athletics are a waste of money, has tunnel vision when it comes to sports because he is unable or unwilling to see the other side's position. We conclude, "John is cut off." Contrast this to a person who has a broader perspective, "Jane sees the necessity for sports at the high school level, while recognizing that funding needs to be balanced with other activities. She has a wider view." Jane may well have a position she feels passionately about, but her view of the overall situation is larger than the perspective of someone who can only see one side.

The narrow or expanded view isn't just an attitudinal state; it's an actual visual connection through the sense of sight. When you open up your sense of sight you can actually reduce stress in your system. This is true for the other senses as well. When you do so you will feel more calm.

Let's work on your sense of sight by starting with the following simple exercise. It is meant to open up your sense of sight by expanding your peripheral vision.

Exercise: Tapping into the Big Picture

- Sit comfortably and look straight ahead of you.

- Keeping your head still, move both of your eyes all the way to the left, and see how much you can see.

- Bring your eyes back to center. Breathe.

- Now move your eyes all the way to the right. See as much as you can see to the right.

- Bring them back to center. Breathe.

- Now look up as high as you can. See as much as you can above you.

- Now bring your eyes back to center. Breathe.

- And now look down, all the way down.

- And back to center.

- Breathe.

- Now, look straight ahead of you.

- You have just expanded your vision in four directions. Notice how much more you can see now than you were aware of before you started this exercise.

- Breathe, ground, and feel the calm throughout your body.

Why would expanding your vision be a calming experience? The short answer is that when you are able to relax your eyes, you calm your whole body down because you have opened your peripheral vision and tapped into your parasympathetic nervous system. It all has to do with how the human nervous system works.

Your nervous system has two branches, the sympathetic and the parasympathetic, and each branch serves a different and complementary function. The sympathetic nervous system regulates arousal; it amps you up and keeps you alert. The parasympathetic system regulates relaxation; it calms you down. When a perceived danger is lurking, your sympathetic nervous system kicks in, sounding an alarm and sending warning signals to the brain. Danger! Watch out! Adrenaline flows. Blood starts pumping. Your gut tightens. Your breath shortens. The "fight or flight" response takes over and you either attack the oncoming threat or you run away from it. In contrast, when the danger is passed, your body needs to settle, to be quiet, to rest. That's when the parasympathetic system takes over. We need both systems because they balance one another. If we were on alert all the time (sympathetic) we'd be freaked out, and if we were relaxed all the time (parasympathetic) we'd be flaked out.

How does all of this relate to your eyes and to calming down?

Our sense of vision has two parts, the central vision and the peripheral vision, and each part is hardwired to a different branch of your nervous system. You use your central vision, which is connected to your sympathetic nervous system, to identify what is coming toward you or what is right in front of you. Whether you are staring at a ferocious mountain lion or reading a road sign, when your central vision is turned on, your system is at least somewhat aroused. On the other hand, when you are taking in "the big picture" and your peripheral vision, which is wired to your parasympathetic nervous system, is turned on, you are calming down.

This takes on immediate significance for test takers, since tests require reading, which almost exclusively uses the central vision. Thus, a high, ongoing demand is being placed on your sympathetic nervous system, putting you in a continuous state of arousal. No wonder students report feeling "fried" after they have hit the books for a long time, or during a lengthy exam. When they use their eyes for detailed focus (as in reading), they are actually amping themselves up without even realizing it. Uninterrupted reading for long periods of time is an intense stress-inducing activity. If you have ever felt more edgy while reading a test booklet or when taking a test on a computer, you may believe that the test questions are "making you" nervous. But actually the problem is the strain you are putting on your sympathetic nervous system. You need to give your eyes a break. If you're studying for a test or taking one, you have to rest your eyes occasionally and let your parasympathetic nervous system take over, balance you out, and calm you down. That's what you did in the last exercise.

What we have just done with your eyes you also can do with one or another of your senses, though a bit differently with each one. Open up your sense of smell and taste when you are at the dinner table. Most of us race through our meals. We eat as if we are making a pit stop at the gas station—"Fill 'er up!"— hurrying rather than really savoring the food. The next time you are eating a meal, take the time to taste the different flavors, feel the variety of textures as you chew, and smell the subtle aromas. This is how many Europeans dine. They enjoy their food and the occasion of sharing a meal with others.

Work on your sense of hearing by opening up to the sounds immediately around you (maybe those being made by your own body first). Then hear the sounds in the room, then the sounds just outside of the room, and then the sounds outside of the building and beyond.

Work on your sense of touch by feeling the different textures of your clothes next to your body. How does your shirt or blouse feel next to your arms and chest? What does the fabric of your pants feel like next to your legs? If you are holding a pen or pencil feel its weight and firmness in your hands. (As you are doing this continue to breathe and ground yourself.)

Connecting with your senses is an effective way of staying in the present and not being swept into tension and anxiety. Your senses are always available and are the best tools you have to connect you to the here and now. It is remarkable to me how unaware people are of what is right around them, and how infrequently they actually use their senses to help themselves feel calm.

This tool—sensing—can help you particularly when you are thinking about a challenging situation or in the midst of one or reviewing one that happened in the near or distant past. We start fretting about what's going to happen and imagine the worst; all kinds of other negative scenarios shoot us into the future or yank us back to the past and work us up. Are you worked up? Right. So calm down. Connect through your senses. Right here, right now. Breathe. Be grounded. Do it. It works.

Personal Inventory: Taking Stock

If you own a business and you want it to run successfully you have to take stock periodically. That means stepping back, assessing the situation, and asking questions: what's going well and what needs improvement? where's the surplus and where's the deficit? Since, for our purposes, you are the business and we want you to run successfully, let's pause and take a personal inventory of your habits around being calm.

As I said, habits are either productive or unproductive. Productive habits contribute to your growth and can benefit others. Unproductive habits keep you stuck and don't help you or the people around you. All habits are a series of actions that are repeated over and over again, so we can say that actions themselves are either productive or unproductive.

Before writing this book I conducted a workshop for teens and I asked them about their productive and unproductive actions around being calm. The unproductive teens were a mess: worrying, tensing up, holding everything inside, not getting enough sleep, eating too much junk food, drinking caffeinated beverages, having irregular mealtimes, not exercising enough, taking drugs, being jittery, playing video games excessively, and staying angry. Remember, being calm has to do with what you're doing with your body, so all of the actions just mentioned involve or have a negative effect on the body.

On the other hand, the teens also identified productive actions they take which have a positive effect on the body: getting enough sleep, taking a walk around the block, eating healthy food, having regular mealtimes, exercising, taking breaks, meditation, yoga, caring for a pet, praying, listening to calming music, reading spiritual texts, going for a bike ride, and visualizing calm places in nature.

I want you to take time to reflect on your actions and habits around being calm, particularly if you feel "stressed out" a lot of the time. Start by answering these questions in a journal:

- What are you doing physically that is contributing to your feeling stressed out?

- What are you doing to keep yourself calm?

By keeping an inventory you are taking stock. You're stepping back and looking at what can make your performance—your "business" if you will— more successful.

The three core tools for being calm are breathing, grounding, and sensing, and as you use these tools over and over you will be cultivating the productive habits of being calm. In Chapters eight through eleven I'm going to show you how to take these tools into various real life situations that you face in school, at home, and with your friends.

Right now your main task is to cultivate your awareness and use the tools:

- When are you not calm?

- What's going on in your body then?

- Which tool or tools do you use to calm down?

  - Breathing?

  - Grounding?

  - Sensing?

✔ Quick Check-in: Calm

When you are anticipating a stressful situation or challenge, stop and . . .

- Become aware of your unproductive habits.

  - Are you tense in some part of your body? (shoulders? stomach? jaw?)

  - Are you having anxious thoughts?

  - Are you holding your breath?

- Use the tools to cultivate productive habits.

- Breathe deeply down to your belly and lower back three times. Breathe in through your nose and out through your mouth.

- Ground yourself (feet on the floor, butt and back in the chair).

- Open your senses (see the colors, feel the fabrics, hear the sounds).

- Stay in this state for a few minutes.

- Return to whatever you were doing, staying connected in your body.

When you are in a stressful situation or facing the challenge

► Become aware of your unproductive habits.

   ► Notice when you are not calm (jittery, physical tension, thoughts racing).

► Use the tools to cultivate productive habits.

► Breathe deeply down to your belly and lower back three times. Breathe in through your nose and out through your mouth.

► Ground yourself (feel your feet on the floor, your butt and back in the chair). Release tension.

► Open your senses (feel the fabric of your clothing next to your skin; relax your eyes).

► Return to situation, staying calm and connected in your body.

CHAPTER 6

How to Remain Confident

Tied Up in "NOTS"?

Three teenagers, Tommy, Michele, and Jaycee, shared with me some of their frustrations with school. Tommy talked about his presentation in history class. "I got up in front of the room and all I could think was, 'I'm not as smart as these other kids. They're going to think I'm stupid.' It was hard for me to keep my mind on what I was speaking about." Michele, at her college interview, thought, "I don't really have what it takes to get into this school." As she told me this she sighed, "I didn't show them my best side." Jaycee said that in the final moments of a soccer game, "I started thinking 'What if I mess up now?' and I did."

Tommy, Michele, and Jaycee were all describing one of the worst experiences a person can have: losing self-confidence when you have to do something challenging. At the moment when you have to perform and your mind starts broadcasting negative thoughts, I don't know this . . . I'm not as talented as her . . . I'm so stupid, you're all tied up in negativity—in "nots": I'm not remembering anything. I'm not talented. I'm not smart enough. Of course, all this negativity makes you feel horrible about yourself. The self-doubt kicks up dust loads of fear—that you're going to fail, that people won't like you, or that you don't have what it takes. The anxiety and self-doubt quickly turn into a self-fulfilling prophecy. Suddenly, you can't remember what you studied, you mess up when you have to play the piano, and you start to stutter when you speak to someone. With all this negativity, your stress level soars and your performance suffers, no matter what you're doing and no matter how well prepared you are.

If you want to be successful in your life you need confidence—positive feelings about yourself. You have to believe that you are smart enough, that you do have what it takes to succeed, and that you can show what you know. It's the same self-fulfilling prophecy I mentioned just above, but this time in a positive direction. When you believe in yourself you are much more likely to perform well.

Self-confidence seems mysterious to many people. They think you either have it or you don't. The lucky ones do, but it's mysterious where they get all that confidence. Were they born with it? Was it their upbringing? Is it something they ate? To me, it isn't mysterious at all. In this chapter I'm going to show you that you're not helpless. You will see where confidence comes from and how to find it in yourself. I'll also train you how to retrieve it quickly when you feel it slipping away.

Confidence: It's All in Your Mind

How does confidence fit into our model of the three-legged stool? One of the legs stands for your mind. Your self-confidence is determined in large part by what is going on in your mind. Mind is a big word and the definitions for it vary depending on who is talking about it. Ask a philosopher, a systems analyst, a psychologist, and a clergyman to define "mind" and you will hear different explanations.

To me, as a performance psychologist, the mind is a chatterbox, a personal talk-radio station constantly broadcasting a steady stream of thoughts that compare, encourage, criticize, evaluate, and judge everything inside and outside of you. She's beautiful. This food is terrible. He's an idiot. I love steak. I hate broccoli.

When it comes to your performance at anything, your mind broadcasts an ongoing, often contradictory monologue about yourself: I'm terrible at conversations. I'm good at history. I'll never make the swim team. I always do well at chess. I'm not funny, I've got goofy hair . . . and on it goes.

When your mind produces positive, affirming, encouraging thoughts like I can do this, I've got what it takes, I am making it through, you feel confident. You have faith in yourself. You believe you will succeed. You move ahead, feeling good about yourself. But if your mind is broadcasting negative self-statements, I'm not smart enough, I'll never make it, I'm a loser, then you are swamped in self-doubt. You don't trust yourself. This is utterly distracting, and the deficit of confidence can seriously hurt your ability to perform well in any area of life.

In this chapter, I'm going to train you to make your mind work for you. First, we will examine what confidence actually is. Next we will look at how your mind affects your performance positively and negatively. Finally, I'll show you how to strengthen your mind so it is positive and working for you even in the most challenging situations.

What Is Confidence?

The word confidence is made up of two Latin roots: con, meaning "with," and fidelis, which means "faith" or "trust." A confident person has faith in herself and trusts that she can accomplish the task.

Fidelis has an additional meaning, and that is *loyalty.* We can interpret this to mean that a confident person is also *loyal* to herself. When she's in a difficult situation she doesn't jump ship. She believes she can deal with it and stays with the process right to the end.

If you struggle with self-confidence, you probably have the opposite feeling when facing a challenging situation. When the going gets rough—like on a test—you feel like you want to bolt. I can't handle this. I'm out of here. When you glance around it looks to you like everyone else is fully engaged. They can do it, what's the matter with me? I can tell you, after working with thousands of teenagers over the last thirty-five years, you are projecting onto them a sense of security they probably don't have. Many other students in that room are also fiercely battling negative self-talk. They feel overwhelmed by the test and they wish they were anywhere else but there. They may appear calm and focused, just as you might look like that to them, but inside they also feel like running away.

Wanting to bolt creates a problem because it means your attention isn't fully present. It's on its way out the door, you might say. Your mind, like your body and your spirit, is a key player on your "Team of Three." Your mind has to play its part so that you can win. Whenever you perform—whether it's on a test, speaking in front of your class, on a ball field, or in a discussion with a friend—you need your mind to stand by you, to support and encourage you through thick and thin, not turn against you and undermine the process. When your mind is yelling, "Let me out of here!" it is a way of abandoning you, which we can certainly call a form of disloyalty. You have to train your mind to be loyal, to have faith in your ability, and to trust that you can do the job well.

Negativity and Disconnection

Your self-evaluating, talk-radio mind has two sides: positive and negative. On the positive side you are broadcasting approving and encouraging messages about yourself: I can do it. I've got what it takes. I am good enough. When it's negative, you are sending out disapproving, discouraging, and self-defeating messages: I can't possibly succeed. I don't know what I'm doing. I'm not going to make it.

In mathematics, a negative sign is a minus symbol; it is subtracting, taking away. It lessens the whole. When you are saying negative things about yourself, your mind is subtracting from who you are; it is taking away the possibility that you will be wildly successful. In other words, you are minus-ing yourself. You are disconnecting from the positive side of your mind, the one that wants to support you on your path to be the best you can. A negative mind persists in yanking you off the path into the gutter.

The more negative things you say about yourself (the more you disconnect from the positive side of your mind), the more your stress will build. Remember our basic formula: stress is a function of disconnection. You will feel increasingly disturbed and worried. On a test you will forget what you've studied, and you won't trust your own judgment, making you prone to errors. Clearly, your performance will be severely compromised.

This happened to Scott during his solo trumpet recital. "There was a piece on the program I wasn't sure about. Actually, it was just a couple of hard measures in that piece. The fingering was *really* tricky in those measures. I kept telling myself, 'You're going to mess this up,' and that's exactly what happened. I felt really embarrassed."

Feeling Alone

When you think ill of yourself, you are not only disconnected from anything positive inside of you, but also from people around you who might offer support. Perhaps you are afraid if you tell others what you really feel about yourself you will look stupid and weak in their eyes. You believe that no one will really understand what you're going through. After all, everyone else seems really confident, right? Wrong.

Sometimes it is natural to feel badly about yourself. No one goes through life feeling totally self-assured at every moment. We all go through periods of losing our confidence. Everyone. But maybe you believe you are the only one who thinks he's dumb or a fake, and if anyone else finds out you will be humiliated. Your peers, your teachers, and your parents will think less of you. In some cultures, this is called "losing face." It can trigger a host of unpleasant and embarrassing feelings. So you don't say anything. You keep all your pessimistic thoughts and feelings to yourself.

To avoid the humiliation of being seen, you pull away from others, including people who might support you. But the isolation only causes you to feel even worse about yourself, causing more stress at a critical time when true support from others who care about you could be very helpful. We all need the encouragement that comes from those who are close to us. Without it, we agonize silently and feel lost.

Shaia recently moved to America and a new school. "I can't really talk with anyone," she said, "My English . . . it's not so good. I stay by myself. I'm afraid to talk to anyone." Feeling stuck inside yourself is a sad place to be.

This is how many people feel when they lose confidence in themselves. They feel isolated and immobilized. While it is true that when you are giving an oral presentation, or you are taking a test, or playing a sonata in a recital you are alone, that doesn't mean you have no support. And you are not really stuck—you just feel stuck. When you are doing anything, your mind is there with you and it can act either as your supportive friend, helping your performance along, or as your worst critic, seriously undermining your efforts and causing you to stall and even break down. How you use your mind to talk to yourself makes all the difference.

Awareness First

Throughout this book I'm training you in a two-step process to succeed:

Step 1: Become aware of the signs that your stress is building because you are disconnecting; and

Step 2: Use specific tools to reconnect yourself, lower your stress level, and boost your performance.

In the last chapter we applied this two-step strategy to disconnection in your body. You became aware of the physical signs (tight chest, rapid heartbeat, tense muscles, etc.), and then you learned and practiced the three tools to reconnect yourself physically (breathing, grounding, and sensing).

In this section we are going to apply the same two-step process to your mind. Let's start with your awareness of what is going on there and examine your negative thoughts about yourself.

The Catalog of Negativity

There are several ways our minds broadcast negativity about ourselves, and they all are disconnections from your positive self. They all undermine self-confidence. As you read the descriptions below, see which ones characterize your self-talk when you are facing a test:

1. **You doubt yourself.** Your internal monologue is riddled with sentences that begin with the words *I can't . . . I don't . . .* and *I'm not.* For example, *I'm going to blow this test because even my own father says I'm no good at math.* You doubt your abilities and are caught up in a downward spiral.

2. **You believe there is something wrong with you or that you are a bad person.** These thoughts sound like *I'm a mess. I'm a total loser. I must be defective. No one in my family has ever gotten past high school; the O'Connor's just aren't college material.* You believe that the very fact that you are having these thoughts proves that you are deficient and probably not fixable.

3. **You regret the past.** You are brooding over what you should have done and didn't. *The whole tenth grade was a write-off because I was busy playing with my Xbox. Now I've ruined my whole life. I'll never catch up.* You berate yourself about the opportunities you missed.

4. **You imagine the worst (projecting into the future).** Your negativity extends into the indeterminate future. *I know exactly what's going to happen when I go in to take my SATs. Someone will drop a pencil or scratch his ear and it will throw off my concentration, and then I'll get a bad score and never get into State, just some crappy school—so I should drop out now and take any job I can get.* You feel like you might as well give up.

5. **You feel helpless and alone.** You feel that nothing you can do will change the situation and that no one will help you. *I just don't have a chance against all those kids in the high-powered study groups who egg each other on. All I have is me, and that's not much.* You feel lonely and perhaps desperate.

6. **You fear humiliation and retribution.** You imagine a negative reaction from a parent, teacher, or friend if you perform poorly. You hear them saying (or screaming) something like this: *Son, when I was your age, I never once brought home a grade like this. How do you explain yourself? What! Silence?* This only makes your negative feelings about yourself worse.

7. **You worry that history will repeat itself.** If you have had trouble at a recital or on a test in the past, you are probably thinking, *I messed up the last one royally, so there's no way I can do any better this time. I'd better pick an easier school to get into.*

8. **Your thinking becomes disorganized.** While you are in the performance situation like a test, you find that it doesn't conform to the way you ordered the material in your mind while studying. All sense of organization becomes unglued and loses any consistent pattern it may have had. Your mind feels like a chaotic mess. *Oh man, what is this? I've never seen this before! I don't remember anything! I studied all the wrong stuff. My memory is as full of holes as a pound of Swiss cheese!*

9. **You become superstitious.** You start thinking that the everyday little things in life—the socks you wear, the coffee cup you choose, the way you drive to work—have a direct impact on your performance. *Well, the last time I had a soccer game I took a picture of my girlfriend with me and that relationship didn't work out, whose picture should I take this time?* While this kind of thinking might not seem negative to you, it does indicate that you feel powerless over your performance and that other things are controlling it.

10. **Other possibilities.** Perhaps there is some other way that negativity shows up in your mind. If so, you will have the chance to write it down, and I would like to hear about it. I am cataloging the different ways people feel bad about themselves. Email me directly at drb@sparkavenue.com and let me know any additions you want to make to the list above for future editions of this book.

Your Own Catalog

What is going on in your "chatterbox"? This exercise will develop your awareness of the "less-than" messages your mind produces.

Exercise:
Your Inner Chorus (Negative)

Sit with your feet on the floor and breathe deeply down to your belly.

After you feel quiet, fill in the chart below by following this procedure:

1. For each category below read the question on the right.

2. Close your eyes.

3. See the answer on your "inner screen."

4. Open your eyes.

5. Record your answers in your journal.

NEGATIVE THINKING	What are your negative, self-doubting thoughts about yourself and your performance? What do you say to yourself that starts with "I can't, I don't, or I'm not.
REGRETTING THE PAST	What are three regrets you have about how you prepared or performed before?
IMAGINING THE WORST	State three things you are afraid will happen if your test performance is below par.

FEELING HOPELESS AND HELPLESS	What do you feel hopeless or helpless about in regard to your abilities and performance? List three things.
FEARING HUMILIATION AND RETRIBUTION	Who will be disappointed or angry if you perform poorly on the test? What will they say or do? Name three people.
WORRYING THAT HISTORY WILL REPEAT ITSELF	What unrewarding experiences have you had with tests in the past that you worry you'll have again?
DISORGANIZED THINKING	Describe what happens to your thinking when your thoughts are clouded with negative, self-doubting thoughts?
OTHER FORMS OF NEGATIVITY	Are there any other ways *your* mind broadcasts negativity? If so, write them down.

The Litany Loop

Cherrie is a sophomore at a big city high school. She does well academically (As and Bs) and recently tried out for the cheerleading squad. She was turned down but encouraged to try out again next year. She took the news badly, thinking, "I'm just not good enough. I don't fit into that group. I'm not like those other girls."

I can't . . . I don't . . . I'm not . . . Cherrie's mind was a catalog of painful self-putdowns. That guaranteed her a year of feeling bad about herself and not making the squad when she tried out again. This thinking—the same three sentences—played out over and over again for Cherrie in almost any situation at school. She was trapped in a cycle of unfavorable thinking that began and ended with negative thoughts about herself.

I call this a "litany loop." It's a personal list of fearful outcomes that you repeat over and over again from which there is no escape, and which leads you to fulfill the negative predictions. You tell yourself you aren't good enough to succeed and—surprise—you don't succeed. You believe you can't perform—

and you can't perform. You think you don't have a chance—and you don't seize the chances that come your way. This loop has a quasi-religious flavor (the "litany" part) because you keep repeating it over and over again, as if you are devoted to it. How can you possibly do well when your mind, one of the three key players on your team, is downright devoted to being negative about you and your chances?

If your self-confidence is low, the first step in reversing the process is to become aware of your personal litany loop of negativity. If it's going on behind a curtain, you can't possibly fight it. I have found that we all have our own list of negative self-statements, our own personal repertoire of I can'ts, I don'ts, and I'm nots that start spinning whenever we face a challenging test.

At this point, you have two options:

Option 1. You can keep repeating these sentences, mantra-like, and watch a self-fulfilling prophecy inexorably unfold ("He who believes he will fail, will fail"). This would be akin to going backwards, or at best, standing still and being stuck. Surprisingly, this is what most people default to because it doesn't occur to them that there is an alternative.

Option 2. You can decide, right now, that you want to shift out of this gear-to-nowhere, and learn how to transform these thoughts so your mind can help, not hinder, you.

If you chose Option 1, I can't help you. No one can. You might as well stop reading this book. You are entitled to stay stuck, and don't let anyone tell you differently.

However, since you are reading this book, chances are you'd like to change your mind about yourself. So I strongly encourage you to pick Option 2 and continue on the road to transformation.

To venture out on this path, you must decide right now that negativity is not going to be your companion. Tell yourself clearly and strongly, "I don't want to be stuck in these self-defeating ideas any longer. When one comes up, I will acknowledge it is there, but I won't play into it. I won't fan its fire by repeating it over and over inside my head. I'll remind myself that my 'less-than' thoughts and bad feelings about myself are road signs telling me that I'm disconnecting. As soon as I become aware of them I'll use the tools to reconnect and build my self-confidence."

Stay in the Present

When you are disconnecting in your mind and thinking negatively, you are not only substracting yourself, but you are also taking yourself out of the present moment.

Let's say you are about to take a big test at the end of the week. You think, "I'll never be able to pull this off." What time zone are you in when you're thinking that? Are you in the present? No. Most likely you have one leg in the past, based on your previous disastrous experiences with tests, and one leg in the future, projecting forward into a time when you'll probably fail again. But this present moment is neither the past nor the future. In this moment you can either go down in flames, or, like the phoenix, you can rise from the ashes. You can let yourself slide into the pit of bad feelings and anxiety, or you can tell yourself, *I have the chance to make things different*, right now. Which direction are you going to choose?

The human mind is famous for flip-flopping from the past to the future and then back again. Reverse, fast-forward, reverse, fast-forward, reverse, fast-forward. Imagine doing that to your car over and over. You'll strip the gears and the car will be stuck in your driveway. You can't go anywhere. That's what your negative thinking is doing to your mind. It's immobilizing you.

The truth is that the past is gone. The future hasn't happened yet. The present is the moment of action. It is your field of possibility.

Stay Grounded in Yourself

One of the hidden and usually fatal traps in confidence problems is comparing yourself to other people. This is an unfortunate human failing and if you can nail it when you're a teenager, you are going to be a lot more successful now and for the rest of your life. People are always comparing themselves to others—"She's smarter," "I'm more talented," "He's more handsome," "I've got more money," and on and on. As you know from all the work we've done so far, this is a one-way, dead-end street. Avoid it. You can never be anyone else other than yourself, so stop wasting your time and energy measuring yourself against someone else. The only person you should compare yourself to is *yourself*. If you want to improve in your own performance, evaluate what it is *you* need to do to improve. While you may learn something from watching others, ultimately you will have to do it in your own way, whatever "it" is— whether it's how to ask someone out for a date, or scoring well on a French test, or getting the basketball into the net. Keep your focus on *you* and what you need to do to improve. The following three tools for building your self-confidence are designed to place you firmly in the present.

The Three Tools for Building Confidence

I am going to give you the three key tools through a series of exercises. With guided imagery, I will ask you to close your eyes and then direct you through a sequence of pictures in your imagination. This is the technique of choice used in Sport psychology. Athletes are performing every moment on the field, court, or in the pool. Their confidence is being tested all the time. If it starts to falter, they can't afford to stop the action to talk to their coach or call their counselor; they have to re-strengthen immediately. Guided imagery provides the tools. It's the same thing when you are taking a test. If you land on a difficult item and your confidence starts to slip, you need an "inner toolbox" to strengthen your confidence right away. Guided imagery will train you to do that.

TOOL #1: Confide

Here is the first tool for regaining and strengthening your confidence.

Exercise: Confide in Your Confidant

- Sit in a comfortable position, preferably in a straight-backed chair. Uncross your arms and legs and close your eyes.

- Breathe deeply down to your belly.

- Feel your feet supported by the floor and your legs, butt, and back supported by the chair.

- Choose one of the negative self-statements from your litany loop (page 69) and start repeating it over to yourself (e.g. *I can't perform well on this test*).

- See in your mind's eye what you look like when you are thinking the self-defeating thought. How does that affect your posture? Your facial expression?

- How do you feel: physically? emotionally? spiritually?

- Once you have a clear image of how you look and feel, sweep all of that negativity out to the left.

- Now look into a mirror in front of you. At the moment it is empty.

- Now someone comes into the mirror, someone you can confide in, someone who has confidence in you, someone you trust. It can be a parent, sibling, a relative, a friend, a teacher, or a colleague. It can be someone living or someone who has passed on. It can be a spiritual entity or it can be your highest, best self.

- See the image of this person or entity very clearly. This is your confidant.

- Tell it about the negativity that is going on in your mind. Don't hold back anything.

- Confide what you are thinking in sentences that start with *I can't, I don't,* or *I'm not. (I can't do this. I'm not going to make it. I don't have what it takes.)*

- See the confidant receiving everything you have to say without criticizing, evaluating, or judging you.

- Open your eyes.

Let's explore what just happened.

First, who came into your mirror as your confidant? Here is a short list of those who often appear:

- My highest self

- My sister or brother

- My dad

- My mom

- My girlfriend (or boyfriend)

- Jesus

- Allah

- God

- My grandmother who passed away last year

- My spirit animal

- My guardian angel

- My sixth-grade teacher

This is your confidant, if only for this moment. The next time you use the exercise, the person or entity may change, but trust that this is the best confidant for you to confide in right now.

Sometimes people feel "weird" about who or what appears. Once, when I was doing this exercise with a high-school student and I asked him to see someone in the mirror, tears started flowing from his closed eyes. I stopped the exercise and asked, "What just happened?" He shook his head, "No one is coming into the mirror." He looked sad. I asked, "When you are feeling low, is there anyone you talk to?" He seemed a little embarrassed but after a while admitted that sometimes, when he felt sad, he spoke to his dog, Popeye. "Good," I said, and I encouraged him to use the image of Popeye in the exercise. It showed me that each of us has someone or something special to confide in. Don't judge the choice, just trust it.

Why is confide the first tool in building confidence? Because when you are holding onto and hiding your bad feelings about yourself, you feel terrible. The feelings become very heavy, and, like quicksand, they suck you into despair. But when you confide them, when you let them out, you move away from this disconnected, lonely place. You unload these feelings about yourself to someone who will not judge or criticize you. That is why we have priests, ministers, rabbis, elders, counselors, and therapists to talk with. They are people we can talk to about our bad feelings without being judged. We can finally unload all that negative self-talk.

Once you've confided, you are ready for the second tool.

TOOL #2: Reflect

Let's continue with the imagery exercise.

Exercise: Receiving the Positive Reflection

- Sit comfortably, with your back well supported.

- Breathe deeply and ground yourself.

- Close your eyes.

- See your confidant in the mirror.

- Your confidant, who has just heard your negative thoughts and feelings, now responds. It reflects back to you something accurate and positive about yourself in response to what you confided. It speaks to you in sentences that start with, *You can . . . You do . . .* and *You are . . .* Listen to what it is saying to you and receive the positive reflection.

- Thank the confidant for its support. (Remember *"Thank You"* from the last chapter?).

- Breathe in and out.

- Open your eyes.

This is the second tool: *reflect.* Let's explore it together.

First, what did the image in the mirror reflect back to you? Contemplate it for a moment and write it in your journal.

Here are some of the things mirrors reflect back to my clients and students:

- "You are capable, jump in!"

- "Don't give me that negative stuff. I've seen you do this before."

- "You can figure out what to do if you get stuck."

- "You have what it takes."

- "You are able to succeed, you've done it before."

- "You can do well because you've worked hard."

- "You do know what you need to know."

- "You are smart enough."

This tool—*reflect*—is necessary for two reasons.

First, when the mind is stuck in negative feelings we completely forget about our genuinely positive and potentially helpful inner voices. We actually have two voices inside of us: one that is positive and encouraging and one that is negative and hurtful. Why are we always stuck listening to the discouraging voice? Mostly, it's a matter of habit. Though I believe we are all born with the potential to feel good about ourselves, there are, unfortunately, forces that negate and disempower us. In our culture and in our personal lives, they often hold more sway than those that help us build a strong inner confidence and competency.

Remember what I said earlier about the media? Turn on the television any time of day or night and it is filled with messages that are basically negative—the reason you need this car, that shampoo, these clothes, that HDTV is that you are not good enough as you are. All too often, schools reinforce this negativity with their constant competition and comparison. Rather than nurture the positive messages, they inundate children, teenagers and young adults with the message, "You are not good enough." If you keep dwelling on the negative, you are bound to feel terrible about yourself. Remember: negative in mathematics is less than zero.

You are not less than zero.

You need to have reflected back to yourself the positive things that you may have forgotten or that you don't pay attention to, either not enough or not at all. You need to hear positive, affirming things about yourself so you can feel empowered.

The tool of positive reflection is important for another reason. It has to do with what I call "psychic nutrition." When you feed on self-putdowns, inside it's like you are eating all kinds of horrible, non-nutritive garbage. I can't do this . . . I'm not like that . . . I don't have what it takes . . . This kind of thinking is totally toxic. Imagine picking up a rotting piece of meat and taking a bite out of it. You will wreak havoc on your digestive system. It's poison! Don't do it!

But that is exactly what you are doing when you repeat the long litany of why you can't, don't, or aren't. Stop shoving the wrong stuff into your mind. Stop the diet of negativity. It will only frighten and hurt you.

I want to emphasize that the mirror is reflecting something that is accurate and positive about you. It is not saying, You're the best in the world. You're a super hero. You can do no wrong. Those kinds of global statements are mindless ways of pumping yourself up artificially. Accurate and positive means the mirror is specifically zeroing in on something about you that it knows to be true, something already proven, something that you have forgotten because you were stuck feeding on all that negativity.

Hearing and receiving the positive reflection is a big step in correcting your psychic diet. If you want to be happy about yourself and robust in your performance, start feeding yourself positive self-statements. It's like feeding your body healthy soups and salads. Building a diet of positive thoughts about yourself will strengthen you when you face any challenge, particularly tests.

Once you have started correcting your "mental eating habits," you are ready for the last tool to help you build your confidence.

TOOL #3: Envision the Steps to Confidence

Confidence is the faith or trust in yourself that is built on what you *do*—on actions not just on what you say. The third tool addresses the need for action. Such action must first take place in your mind. In other words, you have to *see* yourself doing what you thought you could not do. With this tool you will envision yourself being successful. You will cultivate an inner image that will help you think and feel better about yourself. You will use your imagination as the springboard to successful action.

Let's continue with our imagery exercise. This is the third tool to build self-confidence.

Exercise: Envisioning the Small, Manageable Steps

- Sit comfortably and close your eyes.
- Breathe deeply and feel yourself connected to the chair and floor.

- You have just confided your negativity in the confidant. The confidant has reflected to you accurate, positive things about yourself, and you have thanked it for that.

- Breathe out and let the image of your confidant dissolve.

- Now see and feel yourself taking a series of small, manageable steps to correct the original negativity.

- Envision each small step in detail. See yourself taking each one successfully. It doesn't matter how small it is—what is important is that it is manageable and that you see yourself taking each one successfully.

- Breathe out. Open your eyes.

What is this tool all about, and why is it necessary?

Confidence is built on knowing you can *do* something, and everything you do can be broken up into small, manageable steps. Look at how a baby learns to walk. First she turns over, and then, on all fours, starts to crawl. Next, she holds on and takes little steps. Finally, she lets go and starts to walk. This is the same process we go through with everything in life, even though we usually don't notice it.

This tool is not actually about taking the steps. That will come up in the next chapter on Focus. This tool is about envisioning them, laying the groundwork. In other words, you are engaging your imagination to see yourself successfully taking each individual step in the direction of your goal. This is necessary because everything takes place in the imagination first. Look around you. Everything you see—the table, your chair, the computer, your clothes, the light bulb, this book—all happened in someone's imagination first, long before it became manifest in the physical world. It's the same thing when you have to take a test. First, you must define in your imagination the small, manageable steps to succeed. Then you have to envision yourself taking them, one at a time, with your imagination paving the way. This is how your confidence will gain strength. Having a vision of yourself as a success breeds the feeling that you really can succeed. What's more, positive images are like deposits in your optimism bank. The more you have saved up, the richer you are, and the more you have to draw on when something challenges you.

If you have a history of negative thinking, failing, or under-performing in any way and then beating yourself up, you have to change your pattern. This starts in your imagination. You have to see yourself being successful. *Envision it.* Once your imagination is ignited and you see yourself taking each small, manageable step to your goal, then you can open your eyes and move ahead with gusto and enthusiasm.

Personal Inventory: Taking Stock

As we did in the last chapter, let's pause and take stock. This time we're looking at your productive and unproductive habits around confidence. Habits related to confidence have to do with your thinking: what are you telling yourself about yourself on a repeated basis? Taking stock will help you heighten your awareness, especially when you slip into an unproductive habit, so you can turn it around quickly.

Unproductive habits include:

- Frequent self-putdowns. *I'm a loser. I don't have what it takes.*

- Predicting a negative future. *I'll never be good at this. I'm hopeless. I'm not going to even try.*

- Perfectionist thinking. *I have to do this perfectly.*

- Frequent comparisons to others. *Steve is really cool, I'm a loser. Barbara is beautiful, I'm not. Joey is smart, I'm stupid.*

- Not speaking up for yourself because you're afraid people won't like you. *If I say what I really feel everyone will think I'm a jerk.*

Productive habits involve a different kind of thinking:

- Appreciating yourself for your good qualities. *I'm a good listener. I care about other people.*

- Taking risks. *I'll give this a try. If I mess up it's not the end of the world.*

- Learning from your mistakes. *OK, I messed up. I see what I did wrong. I'll take care not to do it the next time.*

- Valuing your opinions. *This is important to me. I need to say something even if it's hard for others to hear.*

To become confident you have to transform your mind. First, you must become more aware of the negativity going on in your head. What do you keep saying over and over to yourself that puts you down? What disconnects you from the positive side of your self?

Next, to get out of being stuck in self-defeating thoughts, use the three tools. First, practice letting go of the negative thinking (confide) by telling the negative thoughts to your inner confidant. Now you are in a position to receive the positive voice (reflect). This will give you the clarity and strength to move forward. Finally, you envision yourself moving ahead successfully by taking small, manageable steps toward confidence.

The three Confidence tools help you stay connected to the positive side of your mind so you can be self-supportive and encouraging. Your stress will go down and your performance will go up. This is not rocket science. It's a matter of steady, determined self-effort and practice. You can't use the tools just once and expect, *Presto! Change-o!* you will become a confident person. Like anything good in life, you have to work for it. You become aware that your confidence is starting to slip and you correct your course. You use the three tools before the stress becomes unmanageable.

Remember: no one wins saying, "No, I can't."

✔ Quick Check-in: Confidence

When you are anticipating a challenging or stressful situation

Become Aware
- ➤ Are you feeding yourself negative self-statements?
- ➤ Can you identify them? Write them down.

Use the Tools
- ➤ **Confide** your negativity in the confidant.
- ➤ The confidant will **reflect** your positive qualities back to you. See the reflection.
- ➤ **Envision** yourself taking small, manageable steps.
- ➤ Return to studying, staying connected in your positive mind.

When you are taking a test...

Become Aware

- Notice the negative things you are saying about yourself and that your confidence is slipping.
- Breathe, ground, and sense (from the chapter on Calm).

Use the Tools

- **Confide** your negativity about the item you're on to your confidant.
- Hear the confidant *reflect* back something accurate and positive about you.
- **Envision** the small, manageable steps you have to take right now to answer the question in front of you.
- Open your eyes and return to answering the question, staying connected in your positive, supportive mind.

Reality
Check

Let's take a short pause. We're about to get into territory that's both rewarding and challenging, and I'd like to reflect a little with you on where we're going.

In the previous two chapters, we've been working on your body and your mind. In the next chapter, we'll be working on your spirit. As you'll read in the pages that follow, "spirit" is a tricky word and a subject that is not usually or comfortably addressed. This is because, over the centuries, the word has taken on so many different meanings and connotations in countries and cultures around the world. Added to that, for most people, "spirit" falls outside of the world of science, which emphasizes what we can see and prove, and tends to devalue, or even dismiss, what we can't.

As a performance psychologist I've come to recognize that spirit is a key element of the human makeup and it is not tied to any one culture or country or religious tradition. I've seen—in myself and others—that spirit has a deep effect on how we handle challenges, how we deal with stress, and ultimately on how we perform.

In working with you on the subject of spirit, I want you to know that I am not going to challenge your religion, your belief system, or your tradition, whatever that might be. And, if you don't practice in any particular religious tradition or subscribe to any belief system, I'm not going to suggest that you start doing so.

I do want you to recognize that spirit is the driving force for each of us. If you've ever felt charged up with anticipation about something, whether it's an athletic competition, a stage performance, a biology test, a date, or Christmas morning or Chanukah lights, that's your spirit working. It's intimately tied into your goals—what you want for yourself—and what you do to achieve them. Your spirit is tied to your path through life.

In most of our schools we don't address the subject of spirit, yet I believe it drives, and is the foundation of all of human performance.

If you really want to be successful, pay close attention to this next chapter.

CHAPTER 7

How to Stay Focused

If you really want to succeed in life you have to learn to stay focused. Many adults have a hard time with this. I'm not surprised. Why? Because they never really learned to focus as a teenager. If you want to ensure your success now and in the future pay close attention to this chapter.

Being focused means having goals that matter to you and staying on track, consistently moving towards them. It's what the best performers do—they stay focused. Picture an NBA player about to sink a foul shot, standing with his toes to the line. In the midst of screaming fans and glaring lights, he targets his attention onto the basket and scores the point. All top athletes spend years training hard and suffering broken bones and pulled muscles to go for the gold. Athletes offer great examples of focusing because we watch the intensity of their attention live on TV. We cheer when they win and cry when they lose. They show us what it means to stay fully connected to actions and to goals.

This, of course, is true of successful people in any field. Consider a brain surgeon who is removing a minuscule, life-threatening lesion from the left frontal lobe of a six-year-old child. The doctor cannot let her attention wander for a nanosecond since the tiniest lapse could result in her patient never speaking again. What does she have in common with the athlete? She is deeply dedicated to her work. She never loses sight of her goal. Every successful lawyer, dentist, artist, doctor, and business person spends years cultivating his or her skills. Whenever they stumble, which everyone does, they pick themselves up and get back on course. To succeed at the virtually unending series of challenges that their work presents, these people have to stay focused.

Focus is the third leg of our performance model—the three-legged stool. Of the three legs, Focus is unique because without it you will not get anywhere in life. When you're facing a challenging situation and you aren't calm, you can always hold your breath and tough it out. If your confidence is shaky, you can use sheer willpower to blast yourself through. But you cannot in any way compensate for not having a goal or for being distracted. If you aren't focused—if your attention isn't one-pointed—your performance will suffer.

According to the dictionary, *focus* has a two-pronged definition. As a noun: "the center of interest or activity." Think of the bull's-eye in the very middle of a dartboard. As a verb: "to direct toward a particular point or purpose." Think of throwing the dart directly to this point. In regard to challenges in life, *focus* is also a noun and a verb. There is a goal of a successful outcome, and there is working toward that goal.

Goals Come from Your Spirit

Being focused is, ultimately and intimately, linked to a very powerful source within you—your spirit. Your goals might engage your body and your mind, but they originate in another part of you. Some people call this their soul, God, Goddess, or Higher Power. In this book, I will call it your spirit or highest purpose. Think of spirit as your power generator. It produces the energy that sparks every one of your achievements.

Throughout history, spirit has moved men and women to become great leaders, scientists, poets, musicians, and athletes. Mahatma Gandhi envisioned an independent India, and then secured it through a nationwide movement of nonviolence. Marie Curie hypothesized the existence of atomic properties and then discovered their structure. Lord Byron conceived and then wrote sensuous love poetry. Mozart imagined glorious music and then scored stupendous operas. As a kid, Michael Jordan wanted to be a great basketball player, so he cultivated his talent for years, on a daily basis, and ended up winning six NBA Championships, becoming one of the greatest, if not the greatest, players of all time.

Your spirit expresses itself as your deepest goals and as the determination to do whatever it takes to achieve them. Spirit has the same Latin root as the word "inspire." It is *inspirare*, which means to breathe. I always talk about our goals as the way in which spirit breathes through us. When people, like those mentioned above, allow this to happen, we say they are inspired. They also happen to be stimulated, animated, and invigorated.

This is true for all of us. Think of a time when you had a goal that you were determined to reach and you worked doggedly toward it. Maybe you wanted to learn to ice skate or bake a pie, or ace your chemistry test. Remember what it felt like when you were so highly focused? Chances are you felt enlivened, enthused, and satisfied.

When you are focused, you still have to put a great deal of effort into the activity. Focusing doesn't take the work out of work. But there is a payoff, and it doesn't just come at the finish line. During the process, you feel fulfilled because you've got a goal and are fully engaged in achieving it, which means you are satisfying your spirit at every step. You don't necessarily have to be "religious" or "spiritual" as a person to get this, though that can help. You just have to understand that your spirit is your driving force and learn how to stay connected to it. Then, whenever you are moving closer to your goal you will feel stronger and your life will be more organized and less chaotic.

The opposite occurs when you are cut off from your spirit. If you don't have a goal, or if your goal is really someone else's, life feels meaningless and aimless. Yet just *having* a goal is not enough; you also need to keep working toward it. If you're repeatedly distracted you'll end up feeling like you're going around in circles. You'll become deflated and discouraged.

How do you stay connected to your spirit? First you set goals that are important to you.

Is It Your Goal?

Recently, two anxious parents brought their sixteen-year-old daughter in for a consultation. Allie was a bright high-school senior, an ace tennis player with a 3.5 GPA. But on her first try at the SAT, her scores were dismal. With her parents present in my office, I asked Allie, "Why are you here?" She responded quickly, "Because my mother wants me to get higher SAT scores."

"Wow," I thought, "that's refreshing—a kid who tells the truth right in front of her parents." When I shot a glance in their direction, I saw that their jaws had dropped. Perhaps this was a little *too* much honesty. Then the kid trumped herself. With a coy smile aimed deliberately at me, she added, "And . . . I don't want to work for it."

There was a pause. We had just moved from refreshing to cold, hard fact. Now, everyone was wondering how I would respond to *that*. I thought about it for a second, then reached behind my chair and pulled out a small jar filled with gold glitter. I shook it up and down and said, "See this Allie? I call this

'Magic Dust.' Why don't you take it home and sprinkle it on your head every night until your next try at the SAT. Maybe the magic will work and your scores will go up. This way, you can hang out with your friends and watch TV, and you won't have to do any work and maybe you'll still score high on the SAT. Think of the money your parents will save by not bringing you to see me!"

Allie laughed. She got it immediately. There is no magic dust that majestically delivers people to their desired goal. They have to work for it. Not only that, the goal has to be their own, not their mother's or their Uncle Steve's. Although Allie was resistant at first, she was a smart girl and not easily fooled even by her own folly. Instead of staying locked in a fruitless battle with her mother, she realized that going to a good college was *her* goal, and that higher SAT scores were necessary if she was going to end up there. When she identified the greater goal as her own, her spirit kicked in: she felt motivated, she did the work, and the next time she took the SAT her scores improved considerably.

Developing your own goals as a teenager is a process. When you're a teenager, many of your goals are likely to be "parent driven," meaning that your parents, in large part, are directing your life. Even if you chose to try out for the football team, or learn to play the piano, or join the science club, there may well have been a parent behind that choice saying you *should* join a team or club or play an instrument. And if it wasn't a parent behind your choice it may have been a teacher, or a counselor, or the culture itself. After all, it's a known fact that if you want to beef up your college applications you need to rack up good extracurricular activities.

But as you grow through your teenage years, there's a shift. Your goals start to become *self*-driven. You begin asking yourself questions: "What do *I* want to do? What job do *I* want to have? Where do *I* want to go to college? What contribution do *I* want to make?" This means you are defining and pursuing your own goals. Why is this important? Because your parents or teachers are not going to be there for the rest of your life telling you what to do. They've got their own lives to live, and ultimately, you are responsible for *yours*.

Unless a goal is yours, chances are you're not going to work for it. Why should you? It's not what *you* want. If someone else is driving your agenda you might make a half-hearted effort now and then, but only when that person (usually your parent, maybe a teacher) is nagging you. After a while, both of you are going to get tired of this scenario and there will be a breakdown. You will feel resentful, they will be angry; you will lose interest and stop working, they'll pull rank and wallop you with negative consequences. None of this is *fun*. If your primary reason for wanting to succeed at anything in your life is to get your parents off your back, you'd better return to the drawing board. *Your* drawing board. You have to want to succeed, for *yourself*.

What Are Your Goals?

Let's hang out here and consider your goals. I suggest you think of them in three categories:

1. Day-to-day goals,

2. Yearly goals, and

3. Life goals.

Examples of day-to-day goals are pass the biology final, learn the Bach prelude, save up for car insurance, find a dress for the prom, improve your Spanish. A yearly goal might be—say for your junior year in high school—to improve your GPA by a specific percentage as you get ready for college or job applications. Life goals are those which move you forward on your path: where am I going to go to high school? Am I going to go to college? What occupation do I want to pursue? Do I want to start a family one day?

For the moment, let's work on your day-to-day goals. This is a good place to start because when you learn to stay focused on your daily goals and enjoy the satisfaction of consistently reaching them you will want to achieve your longer range goals, and you will know you have what it takes to accomplish them.

Think about your life right now and write down three different goals you have at this moment. They can be from one area of your life (like school) or three different areas (school, home, sports). Whatever they are, make sure they are yours. As you work through the next sections use your own goals to apply the suggestions I'll be giving to you.

⬤···◖ Exercise:
Your Goals

First, make a chart that looks like this:

MY GOALS	MINE?	SOMEONE ELSE'S?
1.		
2.		
3.		

In the first column on the left, list three of your day-to-day goals. In the middle column, answer the question: Is this goal mine? (Yes/No) If no, and it's someone else's, list their name ("My mom," "My dad," "My teacher") in the column on the right. For every goal you identify as someone else's, close your eyes, breathe out, and ask yourself, "What is it about this goal that I can make my own? What is it about this goal that I can make important to *me*?" When you've done that, open your eyes and continue to the next section.

Consider How You Are Going to Get There

Even the clearest of goals is just a starting point, not a delivery system. Having the goal of passing the biology final may charge your jets, but it doesn't tell you specifically how to meet that goal. You've heard the old saying, "A journey of a thousand miles begins with the first step." To reach your goal you often have to take many steps. That single biology course requires certain steps: reading the text book, keeping your notes in order, passing your midterm, handing in lab reports, and scoring well on your final. Each of these steps is an action step, a small goal in and of itself.

To ensure success, you need a sequence of action steps that lead you to your goal. Formulating your action steps in the right way, then facing the challenge will be less daunting *and* you will be moving always in the right direction. Attaining a goal is not like a hostile takeover. You don't say, "I want to go to Princeton," walk into the university president's office and demand a full four-year scholarship. For any goal, short or long term, you work your way toward your dream, one action step at a time. In the next two sections I'll show you how to do that.

Divide the Work into Action Steps: Make Them SMART

For many people, their goals seem large and overwhelming. Rather than be sucked into the quicksand of despair ("It's too much!"), remember: any goal can be broken down into small, controllable chunks. These are your *action steps*. (And yes, they bear a direct relationship to the "small, manageable steps" you envision in the "Confidence" tools.) What follows is a time-tested process for doing just that. It's called the SMART formula. When your action steps are SMART, they fulfill these criteria:

S	Specific	Your goal is precise and well defined.
M	Measurable	You can gauge whether you reached it or not.
A	Adjustable	You can adapt or modify it if you need to.
R	Realistic	Your goals are attainable given your available time, energy, and resources.
T	Time-based	Whatever goal you set is linked to the clock or calendar.

The whole purpose of this formula is to help you come up with action steps that you can really achieve, that are within the realm of the doable. It takes goal setting out of the "I wish" zone and puts it in the feasible zone. You learn to plot the path to your goals in a way that isn't vague, grandiose, or unreachable. Instead, you will take steps that are precise, reasonable, and attainable.

A good way to see what *not* to do is to look at Hal. Hal was studying for his biology final. His work throughout the semester was in the C+ range. I gave him the action sheet (below) and he filled out his action steps on the left-hand side. On the right-hand side is my evaluation as to whether the step is SMART or not.

Action Sheet for Hal

Subject: Biology final **Today's date:** March 10 **Test date:** April 4

SMART = Specific/Measurable/Adjustable/Realistic/Time-based

HAL'S STATED ACTION STPES	ARE THEY SMART
"REVIEW EVERYTHING."	**SPECIFIC?** As stated, this step is too general and not precise. Big, global, general steps make them feel enormous and overwhelming. They tend to paralyze rather than motivate. This step is not specific.
"SHOW WHAT I KNOW."	**MEASURABLE?** This is a vague statement that could mean anything. You may know a lot, but it won't necessarily be measured on that test. "Show what I know" is not measurable.
"I'LL STUDY EVERY SINGLE DAY FROM 2:00–5:00 PM."	**ADJUSTABLE?** While this looks like an admirable action step, it's not realistic. Everyone knows that unexpected events always intrude, even on the best plans. Right now this step is rigid and not adjustable. Hal is setting himself up for failure.
"I'M AIMING FOR AN A- ON THE TEST."	**REALISTIC?** So far Hal's grades in biology have hovered around a C+. It is not his best subject. In fact it's a struggle for him to keep up. Can Hal reach an A-? Not likely. This step is not even a step—it's a goal, and either way, it's not realistic. Hal is setting himself up for a big disappointment.

"I'LL PRACTICE WITH OLD EXAMS AND WORK ON THEM UNTIL I GET EVERYTHING RIGHT NO MATTER HOW LONG IT TAKES."	TIME-BASED? This might work if Hal had all the time in the world and nothing else to do but prepare for his biology exam. However, he's got tests in other subjects and has the rest of his daily life to tend to as well. All of it takes time. This step is not time-based.

After we talked about his action steps in light of the SMART formula, Hal revised his action sheet. Here's what the new one looked like.

Action Sheet for Hal (revised)

Subject: Biology **Today's date:** March 10 **Test date:** April 4
SMART = Specific/Measurable/Adjustable/Realistic/Time-based

HAL'S ACTION STEPS (REVISED)	ARE THEY SMART?
"REVIEW ONE CHAPTER PER DAY FOR EACH OF THE NEXT FIVE DAYS."	This action step is **specific**. It spells out in precise terms how much Hal is going to accomplish on each day as he prepares for his exam. By being specific, Hal knows what he needs to do and will be certain when he gets it done.
"ON THE PRACTICE QUESTIONS, AIM FOR 80 PERCENT COR-RECT ANSWERS."	Hal is giving himself a clear yardstick for gauging his success. This step is **measurable**. If Hal comes in under this 80 percent, he'll be able to analyze his wrong answers and make the necessary corrections. By reaching this percentage of correct answers, Hal is more likely to achieve the score he wants on the test.
"EACH DAY I'LL REVIEW MY CALENDAR AND PLAN TO STUDY TWO TO THREE HOURS DURING THE DAY. I'LL KEEP THAT STUDY TIME IN ONE CHUNK WHENEVER I CAN."	This step allows for flexibility. Hal recognizes that he needs to study between two and three hours a day, and he's making this step **adjustable** to accommodate his varied calendar.

"I'LL STUDY ENOUGH TO BRING MY GRADE UP TO A B-."	Hal's performance-to-date in biology has been C+. In this step Hal is pushing to do a little bit better without putting too much pressure on himself. This is **realistic**. He is more likely to achieve this grade than one out of his reach.
"WHEN I PRACTICE OLD EXAMS I'LL WORK ON THEM FOR ONE HOUR AND THEN LEAVE AN ADDITIONAL HALF HOUR TO ANALYZE MY ANSWERS."	Hal must balance his exam preparation with the rest of his obligations. By creating a **time-based** action step like this one he will be able to accomplish his study objectives and still have room for his other commitments.

For every goal you have on a day-to-day basis, make your action steps SMART. If you're studying for a test, in the face of a staggering amount of material to study, it will keep you sane if you structure your time and set immediate goals that you can actually fulfill. Also, SMART goals will keep your tasks sorted out, clear, and manageable.

This is as true for tests as it is for other day-to-day goals. Let's take two non-academic examples. Say your parents have given you permission to use the car if you pay for your own insurance. SMART action steps might look like this: (1) calculate how much money you'll have to come up with; (2) ask your parents about the insurance payment schedule (quarterly? twice a year?); (3) figure out how you can make that money—look at what kind of work you can qualify for and take on given your schedule; (4) organize your time so you can get your school work done and also do the part-time job; and (5) stay healthy by getting enough rest.

Another example: say your goal is to choose a dress for the prom. The series of SMART action steps would look like this: (1) decide on the style of dress you want by looking at photographs (or drawing sketches); (2) research where you might buy the dress or purchase a pattern to make it yourself; (3) figure out where the money for all of this is coming from and how you are going to get it (work? loan? your savings?); and (4) make a schedule for all this to happen in good time for the big night.

An important tip: when you put your action steps into words, state what you need *to do*, rather than what you need to *not* do. In other words, make it positive. Negative steps sound punitive and they don't really offer helpful directions. *Don't rush. Don't waste the money! Don't trust your intuition!* These will push your mind to rebel and say, *Don't tell me what to do!* A positive approach makes you feel better and moves you along in the right direction.

Coaching you to use the SMART formula might feel like just another rule that I'm forcing you to use. *Be specific! Be flexible! Be realistic!* Most people don't like rules. But I guarantee you that this is not a rule that demands more of you. It is a SMART template designed to make your life easier.

Dealing with Distraction

At the beginning of the chapter I said that *focus* is a noun and a verb. We've just handled the noun, the point of focus, the goal itself. Now we have to work on the verb—the actions needed to reach the goal. If your action steps are clear, you know what they are. Taking the steps and staying on the path is another matter. You know you have to review a chapter in your history text during your study time tonight. That part of your focus is clear. But what happens when you open the book and actually start working?

I'll tell you what happens: either you do the work and get it done or, if you're like most people, you become distracted. Even with well-defined steps to follow, we all face the problem of distraction. It is the biggest stumbling block to reaching any goal, whether it's day-to-day, year-by-year, or a life goal.

On the Focus leg of the three-legged stool, distraction is Enemy number one. It derails the momentum of that ongoing stream of actions that move you toward your goal. How often have you set out to accomplish something and found that the day has gone by and you spent it doing nonessential little tasks you hadn't planned on and that have nothing to do with your goal? You have a big recital coming up and you haven't practiced for two days. Or, you have to write your college application essay but end up hanging out with your friends at the mall. Or, you have to study for your French final, but you start surfing the App Store online.

Distractions are a direct manifestation of a disconnection from the spirit. If you look up the word *distraction* in the dictionary, you will find three different meanings with a notable interrelationship:

➤ An obstacle to attention;

➤ An entertainment that provokes pleased interest and takes you away from worries and vexations; and

➤ Mental turmoil, derangement

Doesn't this perfectly cover the process of being distracted? First, your attention is diverted. Second, you kind of like it because now you don't have to deal with the work in front of you. Third, there is a build-up of stress because you've let so much time slip by, so now you are anxious or depressed. What started out as a little blip in your attention span ends up as content for a therapy session.

Distraction is your enemy and it will defeat you every time if you let it. If distractions are everyone's scourge, how do you conquer them? To put it another, more positive way, how do you stay connected and keep moving toward your goal? Simple. As we saw in the previous chapters on calming down and being confident you have to do two things: (1) Become aware, as soon as you can, that you are disconnecting; and (2) Use specific tools to reconnect and put yourself back on track.

Cultivate Your Awareness

The key is to nip distraction in the bud before it morphs into something horrendous. You want to be able to cultivate *awareness* that you are becoming distracted as soon as you begin to veer off track. This is important because many people become distracted and they don't even realize it. Their mind is off and running, and an hour later they wake up and say, "Oh, wait a minute, I've stopped listening to the teacher." Other people know they're distracted, but they're in denial about it. They justify going off track by saying, "But I really had to get up from my desk and feed the cat. It wasn't a distraction; it was something that had to be done."

Todd told me he had carved out four hours on Saturday to prepare for his AP History test but was thoroughly depressed when he came to see me on Monday. "I didn't get much done," he said. When I asked him to tell me what he did during those four hours he listed these tasks: texting his girlfriend (three times), feeding the cat, making a sandwich for himself, checking his email, playing with the cat, and even taking a short nap!

It might seem unbelievable to you, too, that Todd gave into all these diversions and that he was blissfully unaware of how unfocused he was; but believe me, in my thirty plus years of coaching people, I have seen this happen time and again. I have heard every conceivable distracting activity that students engage in when they're supposed to be pursuing their goals: whether it be studying for a test or practicing an instrument or fulfilling an obligation around the house. Here is a list I've compiled. These distractions aren't listed in order of rank, but they will give you some idea of what people are up against.

Dr. B's (Nearly) Definitive List of Distracting Activities

Which of These Apply to You?

- Watching TV
- Playing video games
- Hanging out with friends
- Watching YouTube
- Texting
- Going to a bar
- Clipping my nails
- Organizing my desk
- Cleaning my room
- Cleaning the house
- Checking out Facebook
- Daydreaming
- Contemplating my life
- Shopping
- Eating
- Thinking about shopping
- Thinking about eating
- Opening and looking into the fridge
- Tweeting
- Talking on the phone

- Checking my stocks
- Vacuuming
- Going out for a drive
- Going to the movies
- Surfing the web
- Going to the beach
- Listening to music
- Throwing away old papers
- Doing the laundry
- Paying bills
- Messing with my iPod
- Cleaning out my wallet
- Filing papers
- Reading papers and magazines
- Job hunting
- Playing Frisbee
- Shopping online (eBay, etc.)
- Checking and answering email
- Going to the mall

- Worrying about money
- Going to the gym
- Thinking about going to the gym
- Shooting hoops
- Skateboarding
- Playing with my pet
- Watering the plants
- Thinking about sex
- Having sex
- Staring at dead plants
- Picking dead leaves off the plants
- Reading a book
- Making lists
- Complaining
- Wandering around
- Watching re-runs
- Taking a nap

Now add your own little specialties to the list. Do you need another page? Just kidding.

As you went through the list, you probably found points that made you stop and say to yourself, *Yeah, I did take a nap. But I needed to. A girl's gotta rest!* I understand—you need to do some of the things on the list—but *not* when you're supposed to be studying. Taking a planned break is quite different than drifting off and doing something else. If you persist in saying that you cannot avoid these little activities, ask yourself this: "Do I really have to go shopping *right now*? Is it worth sacrificing the security of my future life? Or am I just distracting myself because I don't want to hit the books?"

Often my clients call this "procrastinating" and you would think it was some kind of genetic condition that they were born with and was inherent to their nature. It's not genetic. They weren't born with it. It isn't inherent. And it isn't a disease either, like something you catch from an airborne germ. Procrastination is not something that is happening *to you*. It is something you are *doing*.

Procrastinating, in itself, is an action. It is a fancy word for distracting yourself. You are doing one thing instead of what you should be doing. You are placing your focus on something else instead of on doing what you know you need to be doing to move towards accomplishing your goal. Focusing is all about where you direct your energy and where you train your attention. Procrastinating is about wasting your energy and training your attention on the unimportant.

At this point another issue comes up for many teens: "School is *boring*. I don't want to do the work." I totally get it. School can be very boring. I don't think it should be, but most, unfortunately, think it is. This is a big problem in our educational system, and I will discuss it at length in the next chapter. Right now you have to accept, however grudgingly, that because you are in school you have to do the work. And if you have to do the work you will make life a lot easier for yourself and everyone around you if you stay *focused*.

Learn to recognize that losing connection to your goal by engaging in distractions produces symptoms, the way sniffing and sneezing are symptoms of a cold. When you allow your actions to be diverted from your goal, it shows up as a symptom that you are disconnected from your spirit. That's why it's so important to cultivate awareness that you are being distracted—because it is crucial that you stop and reconnect to your spirit and goals. Let's list some of the symptoms of distraction.

Common Symptoms of Being Distracted

- The distracting activity suddenly feels a lot more important than doing what you're supposed to be doing, say your homework.

- You feel tired and drained after spending all your energy doing other things.

- You are all jittery because in the back of your mind, you know the challenging situation still looming in front of you.

- Your mind is cluttered with thoughts that start with, *I can't handle this . . . I don't know how . . .* and *I'm not sure . . .*

- You aren't just anxious, but you are preoccupied with your anxiety.

- You are beginning to lose faith in yourself because, once again, you haven't followed through on what you said you would do.

- Other people are nagging you, losing faith in you, and questioning your motives.

What are the symptoms that tell you that you've become distracted? List them in your journal.

The awareness that you have grown distracted must come from inside you. If you are waiting for someone else to tell you to get back on track you are depending on an external cue. There are two problems with external cues: first, unless you employ a personal valet or maid, no one is going to be around all the time to monitor you; and second, when someone continually is prodding you (a parent, a teacher, a coach), you are going to feel resistant and angry. No one likes being ordered around.

An *internal* cue, however, is entirely different. It is a thought or emotion of your own that contains the realization, "I'm distracted right now and out of focus. I need to get back on track." And it is essential that you learn to point this out to yourself in a non-judgmental way because if you put yourself down or talk to yourself in a threatening manner (like an angry parent or a frustrated teacher), then you will feel like you are being punished. *Get back to work or else! If you fail this test, I'm going to be furious. You are such a loser. I can't believe you're not studying.* Sound familiar? If you wouldn't talk to a five-year-old this way, don't do it to yourself. In other words, start looking at your negative self-talk, as we dealt with in the last chapter, as a distraction.

If you repeatedly let pleasant or unpleasant tasks or thoughts divert your attention, and then rationalize the detour by saying you don't really have a problem—"This is just my style" is the common refrain—then you are in denial. You *do* have a problem. Maybe distractions and procrastination didn't hamper you much in grade school or even high school because you are smart and, as far as school work is concerned, the material comes easily to you, but by the time you reach college or get a job, you are playing with the big girls and boys. Now you are facing real competition. Once you're out in the world you'll be in the major leagues. No longer will you be able to get away with, *Don't worry. I can control my behavior. I'll get all my work done at the last minute.* For those who haven't managed their procrastination and distraction until then, it is probably ingrained. Deed has become habit, and habits have a way of lasting a lifetime—right into the job market, where goal-oriented, focused people will beat you every time.

By not admitting you have a habit, you are just doing what addicts do: they engage habitually in self-destructive behavior, and they are in denial about it. At some point you will have to face yourself and your behavior and ask yourself, "If I go on like this, am I going to pass my classes? Will I even graduate?" You have to wake up to what you are doing, come clean, and accept the fact that you are distracted from your goals on a continual basis and it is working against you.

This, then, is the first step—awareness. You know that you are becoming distracted and you are willing to face it. Unfortunately, that doesn't necessarily mean you want to change. You still need to answer the question: "Do I *really* want to stop distracting myself and start focusing?" Some people answer "no" to that question because being distracted isn't particularly unpleasant for them; in fact, they like it. When I asked one student how she felt whenever her attention was averted from the task at hand, I expected her to tell me it was frustrating. Instead she happily answered that she felt great, "I'd much rather play with my cat than study." For her, this was an enjoyable amusement. I felt like saying, "Duh, of course it's more fun to tickle Twinkles than study calculus. That's not the point." But I didn't say that. I simply asked her how she felt an hour before test time when she reflected on how much she had procrastinated rather than studied. Her mood dropped precipitously, "I was in a panic, a total mess." And there we have it: it feels good in the moment not to make the effort to concentrate, but the long-term effects can be devastating. Not only did she suffer greatly with anxiety walking into the classroom, but she dreaded facing her parents with poor grades, and she hated disappointing teachers who saw so much potential in her. This student's habits of opting for the pleasant diversion instead of studying was not going to change on its own. She had to transform them.

The Three Tools for Staying Focused

So here's the good news: if you have such a habit and you are willing to work for a change, you are not stuck with the habit. You can break your old, unproductive habits, and you can establish new, useful ones. And if you use the tools I am about to give you, you will improve your chances tremendously. Understanding and using these tools do not require an advanced degree in psychology. They may appear simple—and they are. Yet it never ceases to amaze me that people don't do the simple and obvious things to improve themselves. They just continue to engage in the same old unhelpful, unproductive behaviors and patterns and then think there's some "magic" way to change.

Remember the physics principle, a body in motion stays in motion until it is met with an equal and opposite force? Well, it takes an effort equal to the force of the habit to stop its trajectory. You must actually *do* something different, not just try to stop what you have been doing. Simply stopping will leave a void. If you don't do something else instead, the old habits will automatically rear their ugly heads, fill the void, and spring back into action. What you need is a helpful step-by-step process of changing specific behaviors. Through repetition, this beneficial sequence will become your new habit.

You need to train yourself with the following three tools. That's all it takes— three. You simply have to use them consistently and with determination.

TOOL #1: Stop! Look at What You Are Doing

Let's say you are driving from Miami to New York. You are on the freeway and you believe you are making good time. But your car or motorcycle is actually pointed south instead of north. If you don't stop to ask if you're going the right way, you may end up in Little Havana, not Times Square. To make sure this doesn't happen, the first thing you have to do is stop.

Now imagine that you are in the middle of a test and you are drifting off. It's Friday afternoon and as soon as the test is over you are headed out to the beach for the weekend. How nice. Suddenly, the teacher announces, "Thirty minutes left," and you are jolted back to reality. How much time have you lost fantasizing about the beach and barbecue? Wouldn't it have been better if you had caught yourself drifting off and said, "Wait a minute! The weekend hasn't started yet. My mind is off in the wrong direction"? When you can do this, you stop the process of being distracted and stay in the present.

The following exercise will show you how to use the first tool and stop the distracting activity.

Exercise: Stopping the Distraction

- Sit comfortably in a chair, making sure your back is reasonably straight and your neck and head are upright. Uncross your arms and legs. Rest your feet on the floor and place your hands gently on top of each leg. Breathe out and close your eyes.

- Envision yourself having a goal. Let's say you are taking a test next week, and right now, for the next hour, your goal is to review a particular chapter in an organized and thorough way.

- See yourself working toward your goal. You see your books in front of you and you imagine opening one of them and starting to read the required material.

- Now see yourself becoming distracted. Quite unexpectedly, the face of a friend you haven't seen in a long time pops onto your mental screen. You think, *I wonder what's going on with him?* Warm feelings about your friend flood you for an instant and you reach for your cell phone.

- Now, use the first tool, STOP! You see a stop sign, a stoplight, a hand goes up, or an alarm signal goes off. You stop the distracting activity (picking up the phone). As your hand goes toward the phone, you realize, "I'm starting to go off track. I was studying and now, suddenly, I'm starting to make a phone call." The urge to make the call is strong. You haven't seen your friend in so long. But you muster up a little discipline and tell yourself to "Hold it."

- Once you have stopped the distraction, ask yourself the question, "Is this distraction going to help me reach my goal?" Is calling my friend right now going to help me be better prepared for the test? Clearly, the answer is "No."

- Open your eyes.

This kind of stopping is a discipline that is taught in virtually every spiritual tradition the world over. Why? Because these traditions, especially the ancient ones, have recognized for millennia the tremendous importance of owning your own attention by stopping when you become distracted. If you want to meditate, or pray, or become enlightened, or communicate with the great spirits, or understand the meaning of life, or fulfill your highest purpose—all goals of different spiritual paths—you must be able to control your attention. If it is all over the place, you will get nowhere. Unless you make a conscientious effort to stop becoming caught up in distractions and change direction, you will sink into a lethargic inertia. It is so easy to default to what is easy and immediately pleasing, to just let our attention traipse around in circles aimlessly. Put another way, it's easier to roll downhill than it is to make an effort to climb the hill. But then time passes and life is almost over, and you have drifted further and further downhill, away from your goals.

Stopping the distraction is the first tool. And stopping means *stopping*. It doesn't mean thinking, *I should stop*, once you are already off course and into a distraction. If you have a test tomorrow and you should be studying but find yourself on the phone with your sister and are thinking, *I really ought to get off the phone*, that's not stopping. You either get off the phone or you don't. People confuse these two all the time—the nagging thought, *I should stop*, with actually stopping. To really stop, you have to put the phone down and return to the books.

But why is it so hard to do this one little thing? Think of stopping as a battle between two parts of yourself: the adult and the child. The adult part understands delayed gratification, the meaning of work, the importance of putting in the time for a test, and foregoing pleasures until the studying is done. The child wants instant gratification, playing instead of working, spending time doing fun things, and receiving pleasure now, not later. Children are only interested in what is satisfying right now: eating, playing with toys, sucking on their fingers, hugging Mommy. The child inside you may want a good grade. It might see the value in all the goals the adult has. It just doesn't want to work or sacrifice for them.

Children are cute and adorable—but you are not a child any more. One might be living inside of you, but you aren't the child. You are a growing person who is about to face a challenging situation, and no baby is going to face that challenge or get a good job or put a roof over your head or put food on your table for the rest of your life. The adult part of you is the one who is expected to perform. Children sit back and expect to be taken care of. Unless you have a nice trust fund waiting for you, you cannot afford to let the child inside of you take over. And unless *you* take action, you're going to have someone—whether it's a parent or teacher—breathing down your neck.

To recap, when you become distracted and unfocused use the first tool: ***Stop! and ask yourself, Is this distraction going to help me reach my goal?***

The answer will be "No!"

Now you are ready for the second tool.

TOOL #2: Listen

Stopping the distraction is only the first tool. You need a second tool that will redirect your actions toward your goal. The following exercise will introduce you to the second tool for staying focused.

Exercise:
Listening to Your Spirit

- Sit comfortably in a chair. Breathe in and out and close your eyes.

- Envision yourself having a goal. It can be the same goal you were working on in the last exercise or a different one. Let's say it's to finish studying a chapter.

- See yourself working toward your goal. You see yourself reading and memorizing.

- Now see yourself becoming distracted. The phone rings. You move to pick it up.

- Now use the first tool, stop. You see a stop sign, a stoplight, a hand goes up, or an alarm signal goes off. You stop the distraction. You don't get up from your chair.

- Ask yourself the question, "Is this distraction leading me to my goal?" The answer is "No." You let the call go to voice mail.

- Breathe out.

- Now, use the second tool.

- *Listen to the voice inside that's telling you exactly what you need to do to reconnect with your goal.* Perhaps the voice is saying something like, "Go back to the spot you were reading when the phone rang and continue from there."

- After you listen to the message, open your eyes.

The second tool is to **listen and receive a specific inner direction**. Literally, this means to tune into your inner voice. But when you first try listening, what you'll hear are a lot of voices back and forth. You need to think about what your goal is—let's say, getting your homework done tonight—and listen for how to connect to it, stay focused on it, and tune out the rest. Something inside you knows exactly what you need to be doing right now to get your homework done.

Of course, your homework isn't the most significant goal in your life, but it is important. As such it is connected to your highest self—your spirit—which is operating in even the smallest decisions that are made all along the way as you strive to meet your life goal.

Each one of us has this inner voice offering us helpful, explicit directions all the time, and it doesn't just have to be in an academic setting. You can be deciding what to have for lunch and you hear the voice direct you to "eat something healthy" as you're looking at an apple and an éclair sitting on the table, waiting for you to choose.

In that chorus of voices inside our heads, there are bound to be conflicting messages ("Man, that éclair looks really nice!"). Sometimes everyone seems to be talking at once. I am well aware that some people do things that are hurtful and destructive then say that they were listening to their inner voice. In its mildest form, the negative voice promotes bad habits. It tells people to goof off and avoid responsibility. As it grows darker, it represents the call to addiction, urging people to drink, gamble, be sexually unsafe, and take drugs. In its darkest form, it tells people to lie, cheat, steal, and kill. This, quite plainly, is the voice of evil.

So how can you tell which one to listen to? You must recognize that out of this chorus, only one is connected to your highest self—your spirit—and it takes discrimination to tell which one. Here's a clue:

The voice of your highest self always directs you toward that which is beneficial for you and others, not toward that which causes harm.

The voice of your spirit, your highest self, guides you in taking the next step, the one that's right in front of you, that will lead you toward your true goals in life. Its voice is connected to the light, telling you how to stay aligned with your highest purpose.

To prove which is the voice of your spirit, take the scientific approach. Try it out. If this direction serves to bring you back on track, then it is the voice of your spirit. If it drives you way from your focus, it's not.

After years of coaching people on how to meet their goals, I am convinced that every one of us has this voice and is the benefactor of its signals. Whether we listen to it and follow its direction is another matter altogether.

If you are having trouble grasping what this inner voice is, I'll give you a way of understanding it. Here's what I tell my clients.

First, take the initials to your full name and write them down in big capital letters on a piece of paper. Mine are BBB. What are yours? Write them in your journal.

Next, if you live east of the Mississippi put a **W** in front of your initials, and if you live west of the Mississippi put a **K** in front.

What do you get?

For me, I'm KBBB in California and WBBB in New York.

What does that sound like?

You're right. It's a radio station. It's your own *personal* radio station. That is "the voice." It is your own private frequency, being broadcast to you, inside of you and no one else, 24-7-365, and it's always there to guide you. The mind is like a radio that is constantly switching back and forth between stations. When you turn it on, you'll hear a lot of voices from the various stations, but only one of them is your own personal radio station that broadcasts from your spirit.

When you set your dial squarely on your own frequency, you receive a good clear signal that tells you how to stay focused on what's important in your life, right now. It might be major—telling you to check with your doctor immediately about that uncomfortable feeling in your chest; or it may be minor—prompting you to choose an elective for next semester. Usually, people think about the higher self as the part of themselves that deals with the mega-questions in life like, "Why am I here? What is the meaning of it all?" But life is made up of ordinary activities, and activities involve choices that will lead you in a certain direction—either toward your highest potential or toward a life of stagnation and downright destruction. That's why it is so important to listen to your inner voice during all the little challenges, choices, and tests that come your way. Every decision you make either contributes to your growth or it takes away from your growth.

Listening to this voice isn't always easy. Sometimes we treat it like a snooze alarm—we let it wake us up for a moment, and then, as soon as the going gets tough, we fall back asleep and revert to our old ways.

I mentioned that it wasn't necessarily easy to listen to this voice. But why wouldn't you want to? Clearly it has your best interest at heart. One would think we would all be thrilled to have such free guidance. Naturally, each person has his or her own unique resistance to it, but there are three difficulties I have found to be common to almost everyone.

The first is *entitlement* and it comes in the form of, "Why can't I just do what I want to do? Why do I have to listen to this if it's telling me to take on hardships or to face a task that is frustrating and difficult?" Second, there is the *need to be in control*. "I don't want to follow your guidance. I want to decide for myself."

And the third form of resistance is *apathy*. "Why should I bother," the person says, shrugging his shoulders. "It's useless. I'll never make it anyway."

In all three cases, the person is pushing the voice away and refusing to accept its presence, support, and guidance, partly because he doesn't recognize its importance. It's as if Albert Einstein is trying to tell you something about how the universe works, but you just blow him off.

What do people do when they don't like what the voice says? They start flipping the dial on the radio trying to find a different station—a "better" message. "This is more palatable. This is something I like doing and it will make me feel good right now." Switching tracks might work with your iPod, but it won't work with your spirit. It is good to know, however, that even if you change stations, your spirit will keep right on broadcasting. You may not be tuned into it, but it will never leave you.

Whenever my clients fall prey to this kind of resistance, I ask them, "Who are you really fighting here?" Invariably they realize that when they fight off listening to "the voice," they are not hurting anyone but themselves. Again, this can relate even to the small things. Late at night, sometimes, I'm on my way to bed and haven't brushed my teeth. My inner voice says, "You need to brush and floss," but I respond with, *No, I'm too tired.* The voice tries again, and if I'm really grumpy I say, *Leave me alone! It's just this one time!* But after a few minutes I realize, *Who am I arguing with? Whose teeth are going to rot? If I don't take care of them, who is going to have to sit in the dentist's chair for hours and pay an enormous bill for the privilege?* That's when I listen. It is the question that makes me pay attention.

The point here is this: when you don't listen to the voice of your spirit, you hurt yourself. It doesn't matter if you like what the voice says. It does matter that you hear it and see the inner direction being pointed out to you without arguing with it, making it wrong, or wishing it were different. Just listen. If you really do that one thing, you will recognize its value and appreciate that it is leading you to the right actions.

TOOL #3: Fulfill

Just listening to your inner voice is not enough. You have to follow through by heading in the direction it is telling you to take. In other words, take action in line with your highest self. The third tool then this is: *fulfill your purpose* by visualizing and then taking action on the message you've just received.

This is how I coach my clients to use this tool. This exercise reviews the first two tools and then introduces the new one:

Exercise: Fulfilling Your Purpose

- Close your eyes and breathe in and out three times.

- Imagine your goal. You have to finish reading a novel for an English exam.

- See yourself diligently working toward it. You are highly focused, and you feel enlivened and empowered.

- Now you see yourself become distracted by a desire. You're hungry for ice cream. You want to go to the refrigerator. Immediately use the first tool: Stop! Look what you're doing. Ask yourself: Is this action helping me to reach my goal? Answer: "No."

- Now use the second tool: Listen. Your inner voice is telling you exactly how to get back on track. What does it say? "Stand up. Give your body one good stretch and go back to chapter five."

- Now here is the third tool: Fulfill. *Do what the voice is telling you to do. Act now.* Don't give yourself time to resist. Open your eyes. Stand up. Stretch your arms above your head, take a deep breath, and remember why the goal is important in the larger scheme of things. Now sit down and start reading again.

By reconnecting to your bigger goal, you place the desire of inserting something sweet into your mouth in perspective. It's just a momentary desire. A much deeper form of fulfillment will come from heading in the direction in which your spirit is sending you.

We already discussed why people don't follow their inner voice and instead act out what is in their best interest: sheer resistance. However, there are also reasons why people don't make the effort to follow through on a goal that they already know they want to achieve. One is that they are lured into the easier task of *thinking* about doing something and they never make the transition to actually *doing* it. A famous New Age group leader once told people to "try to pick up a pencil." Naturally, everyone simply picked up the pencil on their desk. Then he said, "No, I didn't tell you to pick it up.

I told you to *try* to pick it up." And so everyone sat there and stared at the pencil and tried, without doing. It's the same thing with endlessly thinking about studying, but not studying, or doing whatever you need to do to reach a goal. In the end, it all boils down to action. You don't score points for thinking about accomplishing a goal. Anyone can do that—lying on the couch, watching cartoons, eating Doritos. You only cross the goal line when you act on your intentions.

Personal Inventory: Taking Stock

Staying focused is a big issue. We live in a worldwide web of distraction (pun intended): television, the Internet, video games, junk food, you name it. And like the fly to the spider, you'll get caught in this web if you don't cultivate the necessary habits to stay focused. The pull to distraction is very strong. But the connection to your highest self is much more empowering and enduring.

Right now, take the time to do a personal inventory for yourself about your productive and unproductive habits. As you read through the lists below, consider which habits you identify with.

Unproductive habits include:

- Not making a plan

- Letting yourself get distracted and staying distracted

- Abandoning your plan if you made one

- Putting things off until the last minute

- Depending on others to keep you responsible

- Knowing what you need to do but doing the opposite instead

- Frequently blaming your distractibility on other people or events

Productive habits look like these:

- Making smart goals

- Doing things on time

- Having a plan and staying with it

- Taking short breaks

- Considering what you want to achieve and owning those goals

- Taking responsibility for your actions

Focusing takes time, determination, and energy. But the payoff is big. You strengthen yourself in the process and you make your dreams come true. The Focus tools will serve you well past your time in school. My youngest brother, Richard, a superb opera singer, is a good example of this. After his training, he set a goal to sing at the Metropolitan Opera in New York City before he was thirty years old. That was his polestar, his focus. Every action he took was directed to his goal and nothing distracted him from it. His higher spirit was calling to him and he listened to it every step of the way. When the best vocal coach in New York City was too busy to work with him, he kept telephoning daily until a space opened up. When he couldn't get an audition, he found a way to convince other important people to hear him. Every roadblock served to strengthen his fortitude and determination even more because he had a clear image of the picture on his seed packet of who he really was. This took years of hard work and many tests of faith, but he stuck with it, and we all rooted for him.

Two months after his twenty-ninth birthday, our family proudly sat in the audience at the Metropolitan Opera house, awaiting his entrance as Zuniga, the captain, in Act I of *Carmen*. When he boldly strode onto the stage to make his impressive debut, we had to contain ourselves from crying out *Bravo! You did it!* even before he sang a note. As the curtain finally came down we stood up and cheered. He made his dream a reality.

When you learn to focus—when your actions are in line with your goals and your goals come from your spirit—you can successfully face any challenge in every area of your life, and you will fulfill your highest potential. The great American philosopher Henry David Thoreau said it passionately in *Walden*; " . . . if one advances confidently in the direction of his dreams, and endeavors to live the life which he has imagined, he will meet with a success unexpected in common hours."

Claim your birthright.

As it says in an ancient, sacred text, "If not now, when?"

✅ Quick Check-in: Focus

When you are anticipating or facing a challenging situation

- Define your goal (make sure it's yours!).

- Specify the action steps you need to take to reach the goal.

Become aware.

- Are you becoming distracted into other activities?

Use the tools.

- **Stop** and look at what you are doing. Ask yourself, "Is this action getting me to my goal?" Admit that you are distracted.

- **Listen** to the inner voice. What specific direction is it giving you?

- **Fulfill** your spirit by taking the action that leads you back to your purpose.

When you are in the challenging situation, become aware.

- Notice that your attention is starting to wander.

Use the tools.

- **Stop** and look at what you are doing. Admit that you are distracted. Ask yourself, "Is this helping me reach my goal?"

- **Listen** to the inner voice. What specific direction is it giving you?

- **Fulfill** your spirit and see yourself taking the action that leads you to reconnect with your goal.

Open your eyes and take action.

We've just completed a major portion of the book, which is your training in becoming more aware of your body, mind, and spirit.

Now you get to see how being calm, confident, and focused works in daily life.

I'm taking a moment to pause here because I want to appreciate you for coming this far. And I want to encourage you strongly to keep going. It's one thing to read about tools; it's quite another to start using them.

There's an old Chinese proverb that goes like this:

I hear and I forget
I see and I remember
I do and I understand.

Real learning comes from *doing*. In the last several chapters we've been doing a lot of my talking and you reading, or in terms of the Chinese proverb, our work together has been about hearing and seeing. Hopefully, you've become more self-observant, which is totally necessary if you're going to create new, productive habits. The real deal is coming: taking *action*.

The next three chapters offer you the chance to look at your unproductive habits in different areas of your life and to seize opportunities to put new, productive habits in place. This is actually a simple process because ultimately it depends on only two things: your growing awareness of when you start slipping into old habits, and your using the nine tools to act in different, productive ways.

With your awareness turned on, and your toolbox in hand, now it's time for the real learning to begin as you actually create more success for yourself in school, at home, and in your social relationships.

CHAPTER 8

Successful in School

How can you apply the principles and tools in this book to your life in school?

I say "your life" because so much goes on in school that sometimes its seems like it *is* your whole life. You can use your time in school to build productive habits that will ensure your success now and in the years to come.

Your days and nights revolve around school. You get up early, sometimes before dawn, maybe you gulp down some breakfast, and then you catch a bus, walk, ride your bike, someone drives you, or you drive yourself to join a lot of other bleary-eyed students and sit in classrooms for the next six hours often feeling like you're forcing yourself to pay attention to your teachers. While you're in school, you are plunged into a social whirl which is academic, interpersonal, personal, emotional, and dramatic. Finally, the last bell rings and off you go to music lessons, team practice, some other extra-curricular activity, or a part-time job. When you finally get home, you still have a pile of homework to do, sometimes until late at night; then, you eventually conk out. A few hours later, you roll out of bed and begin the whole routine all over again.

Of course, keeping this up for weeks and months and years is itself a big challenge, but let's accept that right now your life is about school, and let's turn our attention to key areas where you can be successful by using the nine tools to reduce your stress and improve your performance. What are these key areas? I call them "The Three T's": Time management, Tests, and Teachers. If you're thinking, *Wait a minute, there's a lot more to school than those three things. What about friends? Sports? Clubs? All that stuff goes on in school too,* of course you're right. In chapter twelve we'll deal with the social part of your life. Right now I want us to look at the core of what school is all about, which is work.

Time Management

Jacqui, a high school junior, was preparing for a poetry test in English on the Romantic period. It was Saturday afternoon and the test was scheduled for Monday. Jacqui had a three-hour study stretch ahead of her. What did she do? Here's what she said: "I planned to review all the material, but after taking one look at the stack of books and notes, I thought, 'I can't handle this.' It was way too much. My whole body froze up. I spent so much time deciding how to begin that I barely got anything done." She looked defeated. "I'm terrible at time management."

What Is "Time Management"?

Jacqui's story illustrates something important about time management. Before I tell you what that is, and what Jacqui could have done differently, I want you to do a little work. Since Jacqui was a new client, she didn't know what you know from reading this book. Let's apply what you've learned so far to develop your understanding of time management.

Read through Jacqui's story again and answer the following questions:

- Was she focused? Why not?

- What does Jacqui say that tells you she wasn't confident?

- What words does she use to describe her physical experience?

After you've answered those questions yourself, compare them with my analysis below:

What Jacqui Said	Which Leg of the Stool Was Affected?	Why?
"I planned to review all of the material"	Focus	Jacqui's plan is ambitious but it's not SMART. "Review all the material" is too big a goal.

What Jacqui Said	Which Leg of the Stool Was Affected?	Why?
"I can't handle this"	Confidence	Any thought that starts with *I can't, I don't,* or *I'm not* means your mind is going in a negative direction.
"I froze"	Calm	When you freeze up, you are tensing your muscles and stopping your breath.

Jacqui concluded by saying "I'm not good at time management," but is that really what was going on here?

Time Management Is Self-Management

When I said that Jacqui's story illustrates something about time management, here's what I meant: time management is really *self*-management. You can't tell the clock to wait by saying, "Hey man, hold on! I'm not ready!" No, the clock is ticking and time is passing. Time doesn't need to be managed. You need to manage yourself so that you can effectively use the time available.

That's exactly what Jacqui was *not* doing; she wasn't managing her body, mind, or spirit. To manage yourself so that you can use the available time well, you need to do two things. First, *become aware* of what's going on in your body, mind, and spirit. Second, *use the tools.*

Let's see how self-management would improve time management in Jacqui's case. To help you understand this I'm going to lead you through an exercise.

Exercise: How Would I Do It Differently?

- Close your eyes, Exhale all that disturbs or limits you.

- See Jacqui with her pile of books and notes and three hours ahead of her to study.

- What can you see Jacqui doing so she can manage herself better?

- How can her spirit guide her to reach her goal?

- How can she strengthen her confidence?

- How can she calm herself down?

- See Jacqui using specific tools to change her whole approach to the task of studying. What do you see her doing?

- Breathe out and open your eyes.

Through our work together, Jacqui learned how to become more aware of herself and how to use the tools to be calm, confident and focused. She came back a few weeks later. Here is her report:

> I planned to study on Saturday again—this time it was for math. I had three hours again. Remember what happened last time? I was a mess. But this time I did it differently. First I thought, *What do I want to get done in these three hours?* I knew that simply reviewing the material wasn't SMART. So I broke up the material into manageable chunks and made each one an individual goal. I thought about how long each goal would take, built in a little cushion time for breaks, and wrote down a schedule for myself.
>
> Once I set the schedule I felt better, but I noticed I was still a little jumpy, so I used the calming tools— breathing, grounding, and sensing. They helped a lot.
>
> Then I started in on my plan. But I hit a snag right away with a difficult practice problem. I felt myself starting to freak out, but instead of going in that direction I used the calming tools right away, especially breathing, and then I used the confidence tools.
>
> I confided in my confidant—the best me—by saying *I can't handle this*. It reflected back to me, *I've seen you handle very difficult things before. I know you can handle this.* Then I envisioned myself solving the problem with small manageable steps. I saw myself rereading it again, slowly, and working at it step by step. I opened my eyes and that's exactly what I did. The three hours went by quickly.

When your self-management is in gear, your time management is not a problem. I can hear you saying, "Sure, but what happens when you have so much homework that you can't possibly get it done in the time available no matter how calm, confident, and focused you are?" This is a great question. While I wish some teachers were more realistic about the available time you do have, and that all your time can't be given over to their one subject, I also know that teens (yes, and adults, too) *waste a lot of time.* They get distracted into other activities (texting, TV, video games, you name it). Because they haven't managed themselves well, they start out really frazzled and it's all downhill from there. If you're a championship swimmer you would absolutely not jump into a cold pool without warming up first. If you are a ballet dancer, you would definitely not go on stage without stretching and getting yourself limber first. If you were an attorney, you would most certainly not walk into a courtroom without having thoroughly familiarized yourself with the case and prepared your argument. In other words, effective time management absolutely depends on effective self-management.

What to Do before You Sit Down to Do Homework or Study for a Test

Create your own "warm-up" routine as a series of steps that work best to get yourself calm, confident, and focused *before* you begin studying. Go through the routine each time you sit down to study. Refine or tweak the routine if parts of it get stale or aren't working for you.

Let's revisit the steps of Jacqui's new routine:

Step	What Jacqui Did	What it Helped
1	Determined how much time she had to study	Focus
2	Broke up the material into manageable chunks	Focus
3	Took a few moments to breathe, get grounded, and open up her senses	Calm
4	Used the tools if she felt unsure about something	Confidence

Every student I have coached who has developed a routine and stuck with it has succeeded. Every single one. Why? Because they're doing what every successful person does. They aren't jumping into a cold pool or walking into the courtroom without studying the brief. They're preparing themselves for what lies ahead. If you want to succeed, develop a routine that works for you.

Another Key for Successful Time Management

Here's another key to help you manage your time well: timed study periods and timed breaks. Many students think that the way to study is to sit in a chair and bear down on their books and notes as long as they can. Wrong. Your brain doesn't like that. Pressing your brain into unending service becomes stressful after the first hour. Its efficiency will go down and you'll start to tire. How to resolve this? Not with coffee! Something quite simple: timed study periods and timed breaks.

The research on effective cognitive functioning (how a person best thinks and learns) shows that optimal study spurts of twenty to forty minutes are the ideal amount of time for understanding and retaining information. So taking a break actually helps your performance. As we discussed in chapter five, you must, from time-to-time, engage your parasympathetic nervous system because that calms you down. When you don't take planned, occasional breaks, your sympathetic nervous system—which is all about arousal, anxiety, and the fight-or-flight response—zaps you into burnout mode. Studying for two to three hours nonstop, appears *de rigueur* to serious students, but it is usually counter-productive and it can turn into a chronic drain on the person's available energy.

I tell the students I work with to buy a cheap egg-timer and set it for thirty to forty-five minutes. Work continuously until the timer goes off, then stop and take a five-minute break. In that break do the following: get up, stretch, go to the bathroom if you need to, and open the door or window and breathe in some fresh air. That's it! (Eating, texting, and napping do not go on in short breaks). Set the timer again and go back to work. After three cycles of this (roughly an hour-and-a-half total), take a longer break (fifteen minutes). Now you can have a bite (something small) to eat, or send a single text to one friend. Begin the cycle again. Planning breaks and knowing you are really going to take them is a way of pacing yourself and not burning out. You'll look forward to your breaks as opportunities to relax, to let go. And building the pauses into your study pattern means you don't have to feel guilty about taking breaks. You've done a batch of work and now you deserve a few minutes off. After the break, it feels good to go back to studying knowing that another break will be coming up in a little while.

I have encountered students who don't trust themselves to take breaks because in the past, five minutes led to a half hour, or an hour, or an entire afternoon. After that much time, resistance has set in and they don't want to return to work. They usually say something like, "If I leave my desk and do something else, I'll never go back." Yes, that can happen, but you can train yourself out of that unproductive habit. It is essential to take the breaks and learn to return and hit the books again. If you force long, extended study periods on yourself, your efficiency at taking in information will drop off (usually after forty-five minutes). You feel that you are doing all this against your will and you grow tired and resistant and your short breaks will turn into long naps. The solution? Go out and buy an egg-timer.

As you'll see in the next section, everything we've done so far about time management can be readily applied to taking tests. In fact, the more you manage yourself before you start studying and the more you time out your work and breaks, the better prepared you'll be for tests. And I don't mean just the subject preparation. I mean preparing *yourself* to be calm, confident, and focused. Remember: you are the one taking the test. Master yourself, master the test.

Taking Tests

Mark, a high school junior, is sitting in his math class about to take his fall semester midterm. His anxiety is mounting quickly. He's thinking, *I need a good score on this test. I have to keep my grade up in math for my college applications. There's going to be a lot of questions. Will I finish? Maybe I didn't study enough.*

Like Mark, when you are sitting in a classroom during the final countdown before a test is handed out, a number of things are probably running through your mind. You feel pressured to perform well; you are bringing all of your studying and knowledge to bear at this one time and place, and you have to make a success of it. You know that in a matter of minutes you will have to practice instant recall and quick reasoning. You must answer all these questions in a limited period of time. You realize that forcing your mind to act in a speedy way will hurt your performance. In the past, that tension prompted you to provide the wrong answers, to leave answers out, and to fail to understand some of the questions. You are quite aware, as you look around, that you're in direct competition with everyone else in the room, and you feel isolated in your own anxiety. There is a vague sense of the consequences that await you if you fail: the blow to your self-image, and the negative impact on your future and on your confidence when you take other tests down the line.

When you are in the midst of test anxiety, you know that you've been through it many times before, yet it never seems to get any better. Each time you face the pressure, it seems like the end of the world. And each time, you feel like you're the only one who suffers this way. *Other people probably think this is a breeze. I'll never understand this material. No one else finds it so hard.* The negative thoughts can snowball into outright panic.

Does any of this sound like you? If so, you are one of millions who go through this drama on a daily basis. Let's look at the tools that will help you. I'm going to start with the Focus tools because if you're not focused when you're studying or taking the test, you can never perform at your full potential. Put positively: when you use the tools and stay focused, you can truly do your best.

Use the Focus Tools
When Preparing for a Test

The most stress-producing way you can study for a test is to procrastinate and cram, which is what too many students do. They learn how to handle tests by doing the least amount at the last possible moment. While this seems to work for many people, because it's so stress producing it is the least effective way of preparing yourself for tests. You're always behind the eight ball, always playing catch-up. If this is your style, I vigorously exhort you (I'm pleading here) that you start learning how to prepare in a less-stressed way. Why? Because cram-and-get-through becomes an unproductive habit and quickly turns into a stressed-out style for dealing with challenges in life. Remember, as your stress goes up, your performance goes down.

Cram-and-get-through has a profoundly negative effect on taking tests because we have been conditioned for years to focus on the end product, not the moment we're in. To be successful on a test, you have to be present in the moment, committed and fully engaged in the task at hand. What is *this* question asking of me? This, and no other. Most students have had no real training at this, and suddenly they are expected to be riveted to the material when the test is thrust in front of them. No wonder there is so much anxiety at test time. Obsessing about the goal line causes anxiety because the person isn't thinking about the question in front of him; instead, he is entertaining catastrophic thoughts about what will happen after the test if his answers are wrong. These students just never learned how to focus. They are disconnected.

A good time to train yourself to stay focused and not be derailed by distraction is during your study time. Follow the guidelines we've already discussed in the previous section on time management: set a study goal for yourself and make it SMART. Review that section on SMART goals in chapter seven if you haven't absorbed it.

- Clear your space of distraction: phones off, email off, TV off, music off (unless specific music really helps you stay focused).

- Set your timer for thirty to forty minutes and then study, study, study. Take a short break (five minutes: no big distractions!). Do another round of studying. Take a short break. Repeat the cycle one more time and then take a longer break.

- If you become distracted during your study time, use the tools: *Stop* the distraction (if it's a thought, or something you are doing, or someone who has come into your space). Know that this thought, activity, or person is not helping you to your goal. *Listen* to your inner voice. It will tell you exactly what you need to do to reconnect to your studying. *Fulfill* the direction of the voice: do it!

When you practice using the Focus tools while studying, you are ensuring they will work for you when you take the test.

When You Are Taking a Test

When you take a test, your job is to take the test. This may sound like a "Duh!" to you, but think about it. How often, when you've been taking a test, do you become distracted by other people's movements, or your own thoughts, or the cramps in your belly?

If you use the Focus tools when you study you will be more aware of the ways you become distracted. These are the most common distractions for test takers:

- Unpleasant physical sensations. *My heart is pumping so hard. I can't breathe!*

- Negative thoughts. *I can't handle this! I'm going to fail.*

- Watching other people and thinking about what they are doing. *I bet she understands every question. I wonder how far along he is?*

Your attention needs to be on the question in front of you and nothing else. If you in the middle of an intense play on the soccer field during a crucial game, you wouldn't be scanning the crowd for your friend or your mother. You can't be a distracted player on the field, and you can't be one on a test if you want to do well.

Use the Focus tools: *Stop* the distraction. *Listen* to the voice ("Get back to the question"). *Fulfill* it by taking action (work on the question and answer in a step-by-step fashion). Remember that unpleasant physical sensations and negative self-talk both can become major distractions.

The problem with losing focus on a test is simply that you are losing time, which is flying by whether you are paying attention and answering the questions or not. Once the time is gone, it's gone. And of course, your own perception of lost time creates piercing anxiety, which makes it even harder to focus on the test questions. As all of this occurs, you are becoming more and more disconnected from your spirit. It's as if you have fallen overboard and are drifting out to sea. The boat seems to be moving further away from you as you sink beneath the waves. In addition, when you become distracted on a test, you break your own concentration. This usually has a negative outcome since many tests are actually testing your ability to think through a complex issue in a sustained way.

Because almost every test is timed, test taking is the one situation in which you cannot afford to let your attention wander. The clock is ticking and you have to prove what you know before the examiner tells you to put your pencil down. If your attention wanders, you will lose valuable time, time that you cannot make up later. Consequently, resistance to paying attention hurts your performance. Listening to and following the authority of your own spirit will help you enormously, especially if you practice it during study time; not only are you learning the information for the test, you are training yourself to focus in the right way and learning to use time efficiently. This will be particularly important during the difficult parts of the test when your attention really has to be focused. The more you learn to stay focused during the preparation period, the easier it will be to do when it really counts.

Use "The Wedge"

In my work with teens over the years, I have found that during tests they get very disconnected from their bodies. They tense up and they're not aware of it. Their physical tension builds, their stress goes up, and their performance goes down. Simply by consistently using the calming tools during a test, you can keep your stress level on a more even keel.

Please don't tell me, "I don't have time to breathe on the test." Recently, one student tried that out on me. I paused and looked at him. "No time to breathe?" I think what he meant was, "I don't have time to pay attention to my breathing and to use the Calming tools." My response? You're breathing all the time anyway. You might as well learn to *use* your breath to help you pass a test. It might take a few seconds away from a test question, but it will make a big difference in how you perform overall.

However, if you really think you can't afford to use the tools, at least do this effective exercise, which I call "The Wedge." It's like pressing the "restart" button. It gives you a new spurt of attention and energy, and it takes only a few seconds to learn. Also, it takes even less time to use once you are practiced at it.

●●●◖ Exercise: The Wedge

- As you exhale, close your eyes and let them rest.

- Feel the breath go down the front of your body and into the floor.

- Now breathe in, feeling the breath coming up the back of your body and up to the top of your head.

- When it reaches the top of your head, open your eyes.

The Wedge is great because it combines all three Calming tools—breathing, grounding, and sensing. Consistency is the key: decide that you are going to use the Calming tools (breathing, at least) after every five, ten, or twenty questions. If you study using old exam questions, practice this routine during study time and then carry it into the exam itself.

When the Test Is Over

Maybe when the test is done you're finally treated to a welcome sense of relief, but that may last only a few seconds. Most people walk out of the classroom obsessing over their performance. *Question twenty-three. Did I read that right? Did it mean something completely different than what I thought?* This is a useless activity, of course, and it just reinforces your sense of helplessness because you can't go back and redo it. Your assessment is probably not even accurate because most people don't really remember their answers very well. Anxiety distracts them.

Nevertheless, in your mind you play and replay taking the test, wishing in vain that you could do it again and do it better. Nervously, you ask others how they did, but because people tend to either over-rate or underrate their performance, you never get an accurate picture. Next you start damage control. You begin to strategize how you'll do things differently next time. *I'll start studying sooner. I'll unplug the phone. I'll be nicer to my teacher. I'll improve my study habits. I'll pray to God. I'll give my money to charity.* Maybe you're one of those people who wail to anyone who will listen about how poorly you did so you can gain sympathy and understanding.

Some people, when they go home after a test, feel so badly that they just shut down. In their isolation, catastrophic thoughts flood in. They start planning for the worst. *I'll just have to drop out of school. There's nothing else I can do. Then my parents will make me move out of the house or disown me.*

What's the deal here? The test is over. Past. Done. Carrying on about it is only going to raise your stress level and hurt your performance for whatever is coming next. If you crammed and didn't study enough, if you made careless errors on the test, if you didn't use the tools, then take a deep breath, feel your feet on the floor, close your eyes, and see yourself doing things differently the next time. Learning from your past experience is the only way to deal with past experience. You can't go backwards; you can't do it over again. So stop the drama and pledge that you will take what you learned about yourself and do it differently next time. And when next time comes around, do it differently. Only you can do that. Only you can transform your unproductive habits into productive ones. As the commercial says, "Just do it."

Teachers: Effective or Ineffective?

If you want to succeed in school you need to know how to relate to your teachers. Like everyone else in life, teachers have personalities. They can be friendly or cold, calm or jumpy, lenient or rigid. While it's natural to gravitate to teachers who are friendly, calm, and lenient, don't kid yourself. A warm personality doesn't always mean an effective teacher. At every stage of my education, I had teachers whom I thought at the time were weird or jerky or out-to-lunch. But they were still effective teachers.

In my playbook, an effective teacher is someone who can inspire you to think and ask questions. She is someone who cares about her subject and cares about your learning. I know that too often this is not the case. Sadly, there are too many ineffective teachers in our schools. I'm not here to rag on teachers. Having been one myself for over forty years, I can tell you that next to parenting, being a teacher is arguably one of the hardest jobs in the world. Teachers are, as a rule, underpaid, underappreciated, and overworked. Imagine facing a group of students hour after hour, day after day, and only some of them are really involved.

All that said, some teachers are simply more effective than others. I don't like labeling teachers (or anybody) "good" or "bad" because it's too global. You may think one teacher is "good" while your best friend may think she's "bad." A teacher should be *effective* for as many students as possible. For me, the attributes of effective and ineffective teachers can be summarized in a simple table:

Effective Teachers . . .	Ineffective Teachers . . .
Are inspired by the subject they teach. For them it's an ongoing exploration.	If they are inspired by their subject it doesn't come across. It seems like teaching is "just a job" to them.
Inspire you to think.	Confuse learning with memorizing.
Encourage you to ask questions.	Treat your questions as an inconvenience.
Are looking for the gaps or missteps in your understanding and seeking to fill or correct them.	Gauge your understanding by how many items you got right on a test.
Appreciate students for what they offer.	Put students down in subtle and not-so-subtle ways.
Are moderately predictable.	Are unpredictable.
Usually do what they say they're going to do.	Change their minds a lot.
Are mostly organized.	Are disorganized.
Have a sense of humor.	Never crack a smile or get you to laugh.

This list leaves out a vital part of the equation: you, the student. It's hard, and sometimes almost impossible, for a teacher to sustain the effective attributes day after day and year after year if the students are not doing their part. The teacher-student relationship is not just dependent on the teacher. As a student, you have a fourfold responsibility in this partnership: (1) to care about the subject; (2) to be inspired to think and ask questions; (3) to pay attention in class; and (4) to come to class prepared. If you want to have good relationships with your teachers you have to do your part.

Caring about the Subject Matter

In most high schools you have to take certain subjects in each of your four years. Students usually have more choices as they advance to their senior year. They may even have a choice in which teachers they want to have. However your school is organized, you can bet on one thing: you are going to like certain subjects and dislike others, you are going to find some interesting and others boring, and you're going to "get" why you have to take some subjects, but, for other subjects you can't for the life of you know how it's going to help you now or later.

While it would be foolish for me to say to you "You have to find meaning in everything you do," I'm going to say something like that anyway. *You have to find as much meaning as you can in any subject you study in school.* Most regrettably, and in general, our education system is not organized around meaning and understanding as it is about information retrieval and covering the bases. This is unfortunate because it often turns school into a grind for you and your teachers, putting a heavy burden on everyone. You all have to simply get through the stuff. Ugh.

Yet even within this structure, effective teachers will find the light of inspiration and ignite it in their students. But even if your teacher doesn't, you have to find it. In other words, you have to open yourself to what the teacher is teaching however it's being taught.

The question, "Why am I learning this?" is entirely legitimate, and if you can't answer that question yourself, you should ask your teachers. You may not like the answer they give you, but school—and life—are not all about you liking everything. You may not have a clue why learning about the Italian Renaissance is meaningful, or why you need to know how quadratic equations work. And reading *Jane Eyre* may be the most boring thing you ever did. But I can guarantee that if you go through school with an attitude of "I just have to get through this," that's just what you're going to get: meaningless going-through-the-motions boredom. If you can't figure out why studying history is important (so we appreciate our roots, so we don't repeat the mistakes of the past), or why you need to learn to solve quadratic equations (to refine your attention to detail and to learn sequential thinking), or the purpose of reading classic literature (to reflect on what is universal in the human condition across time)—if you are just going through the motions, then use the Focus tools. Stop! Ask yourself what is your goal? Is it just to get through? If so, that's not enough. School should be more than that. Life should be more than that. So start there: ask the question to yourself and your teacher. *Why is this meaningful? How will this help me?* Don't stop asking yourself and your teachers until you get an answer.

Be Inspired to Think

Teaching means more than simply presenting material. You can receive the material by sitting at home in front of your computer. Just Google any subject, click on one of the thousands of hits that come up, and you'll have material for an infinite number of lifetimes. An effective teacher is not a computer. She is interactive and lively. The Latin root of educator, is *educere*, which means "to bring out, to lead." To do that, the teacher must be inspired. Inspired, which comes from the Latin root *spirare*, means "soul, vigor, breath." When a teacher is inspired she is connected to something deep inside herself (her soul); she is stimulated, animated, and invigorated. This carries over to her interactions with students as she brings them out and leads them. You may well ask, "Bring them out to where? Lead to what?" Simply, to think for themselves and to ask questions. The spark from the teacher lights a fire in the student.

Have you had teachers who inspired you? You may have had several, or just one, or none. If you have, you know just what I'm talking about. Isn't that what most students are referring to when they say they "like" a teacher? Someone who is lively, passionate, and into their subject.

It's great if you have teachers who are inspiring, but not every teacher is. This poses a particular challenge for the student, who has to find interest and meaning in a subject even when a teacher isn't passionate about the material. How do you do that? Simple: think and ask questions. If you start to really *think* about what you are doing when you're studying or researching, your natural curiosity will lead you to ask questions, and the questions will stimulate further thinking. This happened with Donny when he couldn't get interested in Egyptian history. Listen to what he told me at our second session.

I had a project to do about daily life in Egypt, like what people did every day. Really, I thought this was about the most boring thing ever. The teacher wasn't much help. I did what you told me last time and asked myself *why is this meaningful? and how will this help me?* Honestly I wasn't coming up with much. So I started searching the web and found some stuff about what people ate every day. There was a description of their bread, which, apparently, was as hard as rocks. I started to think about this—what it would be like to bite into something so hard and tasteless. I read that sometimes the bread broke their teeth. My own teeth started to ache! I got interested in other stuff, like what else they ate, what they drank, how they cooked, what they did when they finished work. When I started talking to the teacher about this, he told me a bunch of stuff that was really interesting, like how the Egyptians paid for things and what they did when they were sick. I always thought Mr. Widram was kind of boring, but we actually had a good talk.

Donnie's story illustrates two very important points: first, when he started thinking about what he was doing he let go of his "this is boring" attitude and got into the subject. In other words, he got involved with what he was doing rather than suffering through another two hours of tiresome homework. And second, his asking questions actually brought out a side of his teacher that he hadn't seen before. Maybe Mr. Widram was not so effective in front of a class, but one-on-one he came to life. Donnie's shift in attitude about the subject also shifted the way he saw his teacher. The point is, when most teachers see that a student is genuinely interested, the teacher's natural inspiration about the subject will come out. Back to the definition of educator, which really means to "lead forth and bring out," Donnie's story shows that the student can have that effect on the teacher, too. Then teacher and student enter into a relationship of mutuality. The lesson for you is to start thinking about what you're doing rather than groaning, "This is a pain in the butt." In that scenario, the only thing you're going to get out of the experience is a pain in the butt. Get your attention on the material, convey that to the teacher, and see what happens. You may be surprised.

Pay Attention

One of the worst experiences for a teacher is to look out over a class and see her students texting, talking, sleeping, looking out the window, or picking their fingernails. In other words, doing anything other than paying attention to what she's saying. Sometimes this is because she's not effective in capturing the class's attention. But I've sat at the back of classrooms of highly effective teachers and I've observed students doing all sorts of things that have nothing to do with listening. Here's a short list:

- Texting or tweeting each other or someone outside of class
- Sneaking food
- Talking (not even whispering!)
- Braiding hair
- Daydreaming
- Passing notes
- Picking teeth
- Manicuring nails
- Organizing a notebook
- Trying to find something in a backpack
- Sleeping

What's my point? Simply that we live in a culture of distraction. Most people—children, teens, and adults—have a hard time paying attention to what's in front of them. Their minds are jumping around and they're doing all sorts of other things. You could say our entire culture has ADHD.

The bottom line is that when you are in class, *be in class*. Put away the mobile device, stop staring at someone you'd like to date, stop thinking about what you're going to eat for lunch, quit imagining your favorite program tonight on TV, and pay attention to what the teacher is saying. If you're rolling your eyes and thinking, "Dr. B, you have no idea how boring this teacher is!" believe me, I do. Over many years I've worked with and observed hundreds of teachers, and I readily admit some are more engaging than others. But I also have to say that students are often rude, and careless, and copping out on their side of the equation by not paying attention, by simply sitting there and waiting for the bell to ring. As in Donnie's story, I've seen many "boring" teachers come to life when their students become actively involved. It's a two-way street.

If you're attention is wandering in class, bring yourself back to the present. Use the tools. Stop the distraction. Breathe. Ground yourself. Open up your senses (sight, hearing), and start thinking about what the teacher is actually saying. Just like you want someone to pay attention to you, imagine how a teacher feels when he looks out over a class and sees students napping or picking their nails. Hold up your end of the deal.

Come to Class Prepared

One thing that drives teachers nuts is when students come to class unprepared. If you're at home and you're about to watch a movie on TV, you don't have to do much to prepare. Just pop the popcorn, put it in a bowl, throw a slab of butter on it, shake some salt over it, sit down on the couch , grab the remote, and press "On."

School is not TV. Your job as a student is to do the work before you come to class.

I hope you've understood by now that teaching is a relationship between the student and teacher. Each has to do his or her job. A critical part of your job is to come to class prepared. If you have an assignment due, then get it done. If you're supposed to read a chapter of *For Whom the Bell Tolls* so that you can discuss it in class, then read the chapter—and not when you're on the bus to school! Don't kid yourself, most teachers can see right through students when they are ill prepared, just like they can see right through excuses ("The dog ate my . . . [whatever]"). Teachers aren't fooled when students raise their hands to be called on just when the teacher has called on someone else. Remember this: not that long ago, your teachers were sitting right where you are now. They know all the tricks.

When you come to class prepared, it means that you're focused. You had a goal—to get the assignment done—and you took actions to accomplish your goal. You are bringing your contribution to the table. You are showing the teacher that you are involved and responsible, that you care. Hopefully your teacher will pick up on this and respond accordingly. Effective teachers do. But even if your teacher doesn't, you still have to do the work.

And by "do the work," I don't mean at the last minute. As I said earlier in this chapter, an unfortunate by-product of our educational system is that students learn to get the least done at the last possible moment. By the time you're midway through high school you've probably developed an intuitive sense of just how much time you need to accomplish something and you distract yourself up to the last moment. Then, and only then, you cram it all in.

This drives everyone nuts: your parents, your teachers, and ultimately you. Why? Because you're reinforcing an unproductive habit that will play out later with negative consequences when you're in college and the volume of work goes up exponentially, or when you take a job and people are depending on you to be responsible. Instead, cultivate the productive habit of getting the work done first and then doing whatever else you want to do.

Your relationship with your teachers is a critical component of your learning and growth. Sure, we all want to have lively, engaged, interesting, challenging teachers, and it's a gift when we do. But remember everything I've been saying so far in this book holds true here: if you are counting on what's outside of you to make your life work, your life will never work as best as it could. Even the most interesting teacher is only as effective as her students are engaged. Teaching is not a personality contest. It's a relationship between the one who leads—the teacher—and the one who is brought forth. That's you.

CHAPTER 9

Happy at Home

There are all kinds of families. Families with two parents, one parent, straight parents, gay parents, adoptive parents, foster parents, grandparents instead of parents, and older siblings or aunts and uncles acting as parents. Some families have one child, some have nine or more, some none. Each family has its own "emotional landscape" which can be happy, unhappy, supportive and encouraging, unsupportive and discouraging, neglectful, or abusive. (If I haven't mentioned your family, write and tell me about it; my email address is at the end of the book. I'm always discovering new family combinations and dynamics.)

After working with teens and their families for over thirty-five years I have seen some extremely, if not excruciatingly, challenging family environments, from families on welfare struggling to put a decent meal on the table, to families that have full-time cooks. And if you think that the families with no money are the challenging ones, think again. Money does not guarantee happiness. I've worked with kids from very well-off families where there is a deep unhappiness and painful lack of support, and families with the most meager means where love and encouragement blossom every day.

Whatever your family circumstances are, I want you to remember something I said at the beginning of the book and repeated in the last chapter. *The conditions may change, but you always are you.* You are the one who has to function and function well in whatever family environment you are in. So when I titled this chapter "Happy at Home," I appreciate that a more accurate title might have been "As Happy as Possible at Home" because if you're in a family with a lot of ongoing strife, you have an extra challenge on your hands (and if you're in a family where you are lovingly and regularly supported I hope you feel blessed and grateful). Whatever the outer circumstances—your family structure and its emotional landscape—they are yours, and while you can't change them, you can always work on yourself.

In this chapter we're going to work on how you can use the nine tools to be more calm, confident, and focused at home with your family.

It would take an encyclopedia to cover the full range of family situations that teenagers face on a daily basis and for me to show you how to use the tools in all of them. What I believe will help you most is to look at three typical scenarios where keeping yourself calm, confident, and focused will help you be successful at home.

Let's start out with what I mean by "being successful at home." Three things:

1. Communicating clearly.

2. Respecting differences.

3. Contributing to the home.

We'll look at each of these individually and how you can use the tools to achieve them.

Communicating Clearly

Jennie, age fourteen, has just arrived home from school. She's had a bad day. She messed up on her biology quiz, one of her friends dumped her, and she has a huge pile of homework to do. She comes home, stomps past her mom, who's laid out a nice snack for her in the kitchen, goes into her room, and shuts the door. The next day, when Jennie came for a coaching session with me, she said, "I just didn't want to deal with it anyone. No one understands me."

She had good reason to think this: her mom usually tries to talk Jennie out of any less-than-positive feelings by saying things like, "It wasn't that bad," or "Look on the bright side," or "You're always so negative." Jennie doesn't like what her mom says and figures it's no use trying.

Trying what? To change her mom's behavior? We know by now that that's not going to work. Her mom is doing whatever she's doing. That's her mom. It's Jennie that has to change. "How?" she asks me, very warily, thinking I'm going to give her a dose of "don't be so negative."

Since I'm coaching you, the reader, to be calm, confident, and focused, I want you to think through this situation with me and what Jennie can do to make a change.

A good way to start, in any situation, is to look at which "leg" of the stool could use strengthening right now. What would that be in Jennie's case? Let's examine each leg briefly.

Calm. Jennie is definitely not calm. She's had a crappy day and she's upset. Telling herself to "calm down" or attempting to implement the Calming tools is probably not going to work right now. That would be just another version of what her mom tells her ("Look on the bright side. Don't be so negative.").

Confidence. Jennie is sure she knows how her mother is going to react; she's confident in her assessment of the situation and that going right to her room and closing the door is, as she puts it, "the only way to go."

Focus. What is Jennie's goal right now? Simply put: to prove that no one understands her. And what actions does she take to get to her goal? She gives her mom the silent treatment and isolates herself in her room. Jennie has repeated these actions so many times that they've become a habit. Jennie's habit is *when I'm having a bad day, I shut my door.*

As we've been working together we've looked at productive and unproductive habits, and through that lens I'd say this is unproductive: it doesn't lead to any positive outcome and it ends up in disconnection. Remember: *disconnection is the root cause of stress.* At this point Jennie said, "But my mom is the one with the problem, she doesn't listen to me, so what else can I do but close the door?" But Jennie's mom is simply Jennie's mom. Expecting that *Mom* will change is not going to work. So what can *Jennie* do? She can do something very different. She can use the tools to *communicate clearly.*

Here's what the same scenario would look like if Jennie used the tools.

Jennie has had a bad day—the biology quiz, the friend, the homework—and she comes home in a bad mood. Rather than have her goal to prove that no one understands her by stomping through the kitchen (missing the snack!) and shutting her door, she can take on a different goal: to communicate clearly. With this goal she takes the following action: she sits down and says, "I've had a bad day, Mom, and before you say anything, I want you just to listen to what happened to me, OK?"

So, you may well ask, what happens if Jennie goes through all this and Mom says, "You're so negative. Look on the bright side"? Sure, Jennie might want to stomp up to her room, shouting, "I *knew* this would happen. That crazy Dr. B! What was he *thinking*?" Or, she could use the tools.

The first one would be the Calming tool of *breathing*. When something is happening outside of you that you don't like, one of the first things you disconnect is your breath. You just stop breathing without even realizing it and your blood pressure goes up and you want to scream or you want to get out of there. So breathing is first, and quickly *grounding*, too (that will keep Jennie there in the kitchen, not stomping away). She might even use *sensing* by looking at the "bigger picture": actually seeing her mom as someone who really loves her and wants the best for her. In this calm state Jennie can say, "Mom, I really need you just to listen to the things that happened to me today. When you tell me I'm negative, I just want to run up to my room and slam my door."

This is a clear communication. It starts with focus—the goal is to stay connected—and to take actions that get you there. In Jennie's case it would be talking to Mom instead of running away; staying calm, and working things out together instead of feeling and acting that it's hopeless and things will never change.

Where does the confidence leg come in here? Let's run through how to use those tools in this scenario. I ask Jennie to close her eyes and look into a mirror and see her best, brightest, and highest self and tell me what she sees. "I'm standing tall and I'm smiling. I feel good about myself and about everyone." Now I coach her, standing at the mirror, to see herself using the Confidence tools. First, she must *confide* in the image in the mirror, tell it the negativity (and remember this has to be a negative feeling about *yourself*, not someone else). Jennie says, "I can't get my mother to understand me." The mirror then reflects back something accurate and positive. For Jennie it's, "You've explained yourself well to your mom before. You can do it." Now Jennie *envisions* the small manageable steps she can take to correct the negativity. She sees herself changing her goal—to communicate clearly—then she sees herself using the Calming tools, asking her mom to listen, and then telling her mom about her bad day. After this, Jennie opened her eyes and said, "It's true. I can tell my mom what's going on. I can ask her to listen. I can stay calm even if she doesn't do it at first."

Communicating clearly means two things:

1. You say what's going on with you.

2. You say what you need from the other person.

After that, it depends what kind of relationship both people want. In Jennie's case, her mom did want a better connection with Jennie and she was able to listen to Jennie and honor her request not to always jump in and smooth things over.

My hope for all family relationships is that both people would want to keep improving their connection and help it to grow (remember: better connection means less stress and better performance, in this case as a mother-daughter team). Sorry to say, that's not always the case. You might want a better relationship with your mom, or dad, or sister or brother, but they may not. So again, you have to do what *you* can which is to *communicate clearly*.

Remember: shutting down doesn't help. It's a disconnection and it perpetuates the stressful feelings. Sure, you may get angry and need to shut down for a little while till you can calm down and reorient your focus (use the tools!). But once you've made those adjustments, get back into the relationship and communicate clearly. Also, people can't read your mind. If you shut down you are likely expecting that others will just *know* how you feel. Most often they don't. They are busy dealing with all their own stuff. Take responsibility for yourself, stay connected, and communicate clearly.

Respecting Differences

Jennie learned what she needed to do to communicate clearly. But communicating is a two way street. It also involves listening to the other person and responding to what they have to say. In this section you'll learn to use the tools to listen and respond effectively. When you respond, you need to be respectful of the other person and how they might be different than you are.

Mark and his older brother Sam are not getting along. Mark, a high school sophomore, is on the prize-winning debate team and has a 4.0 GPA. Sam, three years older, is a first year student at a local junior college. When he was in high school he was a star basketball player and a B-/C student. Sam puts Mark down all the time calling him a "wuss" and a "brainiac." Mark came into my office, dejected, and said, "Any time I say anything to Sam he makes fun of me. I'm tired of it. I tell him to stop, but he won't. My parents say 'It's between the two of you.' I don't know what I can do differently."

I told Mark that was a good start: thinking of what *he* could do, rather than trying to change his brother. I asked Mark to identify the leg of the stool that could use attention. He was thoughtful, "Well, I'm certainly not calm when Sam calls me names. And I'm not confident that things can change with Sam. Focus? I'm not sure what the focus leg has to do with it."

Mark was right about the Calm and Confidence legs being shaky in his interactions with Sam, and a bit later we talked about how he could use those tools in this challenging, stressful situation. But first, we reviewed what Focus was all about: having a goal and taking actions to get to it. "What's your goal with Sam?" I asked.

"To get him to stop putting me down."

"No," I said, "you just slipped into changing-someone-else-mode."

He smiled, realizing his mistake and took a moment to think. "I guess it's to have a better relationship with my brother."

"Exactly," I said, "let's see what actions can take you to that goal."

So I coached Mark in the steps to have a better relationship with Sam, which he put to use. Here's what he did.

Mark went home and said, "Sam, I'd like to talk with you. I'm not sure you want to talk with me, so I'm going to suggest we have what Dr. B calls 'a dialogue.'"

Sam rolled his eyes on hearing the name Dr. B, knowing that Mark was working with me as his performance coach. "Oh yeah, that *other* brainiac."

Mark let that go and said, "Here's what I'd like us to do. I'm going to start by telling you what I want for our relationship and what's bothering me about it. I'm going to focus on my feelings, not on telling you what to do. You're going to listen. When I finish you're going to repeat what I said. Then we're going to switch it. You're going to tell me what you want and what's bothering you and I'm going to listen and then repeat what you said. Can we do that?"

Sam was moderately interested. He said, "OK."

The Dialogue Setup

The setup of the dialogue is very straightforward. First, you get the other person's agreement to talk, then you explain the ground rules:

1. When Person A talks, Person B listens without making comments, criticisms, or asking questions.

2. Person A talks about himself, *not* about the other person. He uses "I" or "me" statements like "I feel put down when you say, 'You're a wuss,'" (rather than, "You're wrong for putting me down").

3. When Person A is done, Person B repeats exactly what he (or she) heard.

4. Then you reverse the process.

Let's see what happened with Mark and Sam when they did this.

> **Mark:** I would like us to have a closer relationship.
>
> **Sam:** You would like us to have a closer relationship.
>
> **Mark:** I feel put down when you say things to me like, "You're a wuss."
>
> **Sam:** You feel put down then I say things to you like, "You're a wuss."
>
> **Mark:** And when you say that, I don't want to be with you.
>
> **Sam:** And when I say that, you don't want to be with me.

Then Sam got his turn.

> **Sam:** I feel hurt because I don't think you care about me.
>
> **Mark:** You feel hurt because you don't think I care about you.
>
> **Sam:** When you don't come to any of my basketball games I feel angry and hurt.
>
> **Mark:** When I don't come to any of your basketball games you feel angry and hurt.
>
> **Sam:** It would mean a lot to me if you came and cheered me on.
>
> **Mark:** It would mean a lot to you if I came and cheered you on.
>
> **Sam:** I'd like a closer relationship, too.
>
> **Mark:** You'd like a closer relationship, too.

What's happening here? The dialogue gives Mark and Sam a structured and safe place for each of them to express their feelings and know they are being heard. When a person mirrors back to you exactly what you said, you know they "get it."

In the dialogue the two people don't accuse or blame one another. Each person states what's going on for *him*. The format ensures that each person will have a chance to speak and to be listened to without comment or criticism.

Some years ago my wife and I were having trouble com-municating. Anything either of us said got under the other person's skin so quickly that any remark was like lighting a short fuse that immediately triggered an explosion. Talk about an unproductive habit! We knew we needed help. The counselor we went to coached us to have a dialogue. Then she said, "The mark of a good relationship is that each person holds what the other person thinks and feels with equal weight as their own feelings." This isn't easy. We're very quick to think "I'm right and she's wrong." The real deal is "I feel this way, she feels that way. Her feelings are just as 'right' as mine are." In fact, there's no such thing as a "right" feeling because that would imply there's a "wrong" feeling, and no one's feeling is wrong, it's simply *their feeling*.

Just as you want others to respect you—your thoughts, and feelings, and ways of looking at things—you need to respect them. A climate of *mutual respect* for each other's differences means less stress, more acceptance, and better performance as a family.

What tools are we using in the dialogue? Certainly the Focus tools: we have a goal (to have a better relationship) and the dialogue is a sequence of actions that take us to the goal. The Calming tools also come into play. When you listen to the other person you don't flare up, scream, or run out of the room, you *listen*. And while you're listening you can use the tools of breathing, grounding, and sensing. And confidence?

Ultimately, confidence is built on taking small, manageable steps successfully. That's just what you and the other person are doing *together* when you go through the dialogue step-by-step. By having the dialogue you are building your confidence in yourselves ("I can say what I need to say"), each other ("We can listen to each other"), and the relationship ("When we respect one another we have a better relationship"). Remember, the word "confidence" means "trust, loyalty, and belief in." The dialogue is a process of building mutual respect; and by doing so, you trust each other and believe in your possibilities together.

One more thought here. You'll notice I haven't said anything about *agreeing* with each other. This isn't about agreeing. This is about really *hearing* one another and respecting how the other person is different from you. If you have the expectation that everyone should agree with you, please let go of it! Because that means you're thinking "I'm right." Well, guess what? Everybody's thinking that! So let's get a new baseline going: "I have my feelings, thoughts, and reactions just like everyone else has theirs." That's called mutual respect. When you have to *come to an agreement* on some matter—whether it's your curfew, or your allowance, or your diet—communicating clearly and mutual respect will go a long way to finding a solution that works.

Contributing to the Home

Your family, whatever its configuration and whatever its feeling, is a community. Community is not a physical thing. It's more a feeling of connection and of being part of something greater than just yourself. As a beloved teacher of mine once said, "Community is a phenomenon of the spirit. It comes and goes and must be deliberately sought after." One good way to promote the spirit and feeling of community in your family is to contribute to it.

What does "contribute" mean? In a word, it means "giving." Families function best when each person—parents and children—makes a contribution. Unfortunately, for the children in the family this concept has devolved into something called "chores". To me, a "chore" sounds like forced labor. "Did you do your *chores* today?" Grim, boring, required work. Ugh.

While there are all kinds of less-than-gleeful activities to do around the home, from washing the dishes to taking out the garbage, they are necessary for the family and its home to function well. These activities range from the day-to-day requirements just mentioned to more complicated activities like paying bills and earning money to pay the bills. When these things *aren't* done, when there's a lapse, when the dishes pile up, or the bills are not paid, there is a disconnect, and guess what—you should know this by now—disconnection causes stress.

You can help your whole family reduce its stress by making your contribution to the family's well-being. Your contribution should be something that you and others see the value in, even the necessity of, in order for the home to run smoothly and the family to be happier. In other words, your contribution is your way of connecting to your family.

"I don't get it" is the response I get from some teenagers to the point I just made. "I'm already connected. I'm the oldest [youngest, only] child." Yes, that is your *position* in the family. But a position is simply a place in the lineup. I'm talking about something different, an action you can take to build and maintain your family's well being.

Let's see what goes into making a contribution.

First, it needs to be something you can do that genuinely helps the family function better. Whether it's setting the table before dinner and doing the dishes after, or flipping burgers at McDonalds and contributing part of your income to family expenses (or covering your own), there are things you can do to contribute to the family on an ongoing basis. You could leave this up to your parents and let them tell you what to do, but then we're into the whole "chores" thing and that's not what I'm talking about.

This is not about your parents telling or requiring you to do something. This is about you giving to your family.

Look at all of the things that need to be done around in your family and around your home on a daily, weekly, or monthly basis. What can you do to contribute? Here's a short list:

- Keep your own space orderly

- Set the table

- Wash the dishes

- Sweep the floors

- Take out the garbage

- Do the laundry

- Cook a meal

- Babysit (if you have younger siblings)

- Help out with an elderly relative

- Take a part-time job

- Mow the lawn

- Wash the car

- Wash the windows

- Practice your instrument or do your studies without anyone asking

- Clean your room

- Clean your bathroom, including the toilet

- Bake cookies

- Read a story to your younger siblings

- Write a thank-you note to your parents

- Call a grandparent and ask them to tell you about their childhood

- Do errands

- You get the idea . . .

This is hardly an exhaustive list. The point here is to determine what *you* can do. Look at the above list (and anything you might add to it) and, in a family meeting, you can say, "I'd like to . . . " and offer how you can contribute. You can also sit down with your parents and ask them, "What can I do to help out around here?"

I'm suggesting you be proactive for a reason. When you are a teenager, you are building your parents' trust in you. The only way to really build trust is through action, by taking on responsibility and following through with it. Trust is not an idea; it's born of focused action.

So here's where the tools come in. Making a contribution means being *focused*—having a goal and taking actions that lead you to it. Say your goal of contributing means you do the vacuuming around your house or apartment once a week. Following through means you do it without anyone having to remind, cajole, or force you. You are doing it because you committed, you are not distracted. You are responsible to your commitment.

There are other parts to making a contribution. One is to do it happily and willingly. Nothing is worse than someone resenting what they are doing. It makes the air smelly and it is unpleasant for everyone. If you can't find something to contribute willingly and happily, then either find something else that you can do with a different attitude, or *change* your attitude. If you believe you shouldn't have to contribute you're going down the wrong track. No one owes you. You, like your parents, are all members of a team, and you must do your part. Willingly. Happily. And gratefully.

This is the last requirement for making a contribution. Gratitude. It means giving thanks, or, in this case, making your contribution gratefully. You may say, "But shouldn't someone be grateful to *me*, for making a contribution?" Yes, it's nice when that happens (though don't expect it because not everyone shows their gratitude). Making your contribution is a way for you to give thanks. You are thankful for everything you have been given (food, a place to sleep, whatever personal and physical comforts you have), and your contribution is a way of showing how grateful you are.

How do the tools come into your making a contribution? I mentioned earlier that your contribution is an action that takes you to your goal at home, which is to have an easier, happier, and better home life. This is your *focus*. If you pull away and disconnect—"I don't *want* to take out the garbage!" "I'm not going to babysit my little brother"—you are causing stress for yourself and for your family.

As you make your contribution happily, willingly, and gratefully you will find that the Calm tools support you naturally. When you are contributing, keep yourself in the present with your breath, with grounding, and with sensing. This will add to your experience. You will be more present to what you are doing and not just doing it to get it over with.

And the Confidence tools? It may be that because of your past actions, your parents aren't too confident in you being responsible and keeping your word. By making a contribution you are showing, in small, manageable steps, that you are capable and responsible, and that you can be trusted. Isn't that what you *really* want?

Alex's story is helpful here.

I'm supposed to wash and dry the dishes after supper. I used to hate doing it. It was really a pain in the butt. I felt like I had to drag myself through it every night. After Dr. B and I talked about it something changed. First, he told me to pay attention to what I was thinking about while I was doing the dishes. When I did that I realized my mind was everywhere else but on doing the dishes. I was thinking about what friend I was going to text when I finished, how much homework I had, what I wanted to watch on TV I actually wasn't really there.

Then I followed what Dr. B coached me to do and I used the Calming tools. That's when I realized that I wasn't really breathing. Of course I was stressed out! I felt my feet on the floor and opened up my senses, actually feeling that water on my hands, the dishes, the soapsuds. I started to relax into doing the dishes. I know this sounds corny, but this stuff works! I wasn't hating it. The next thing that happened, once I calmed down, was I thought about how fortunate I am to have just eaten a good meal, and to have a family. Sure, sometimes I can't stand my sister (we're working on that), but still, there are a lot of people out there who don't have anything. I didn't have such a bad attitude. This went on the next few nights and I've kept it up. I can't say I love doing the dishes, but I'm not always trying to get out of it either.

When your feelings about what you're doing change, you'll see that other's feelings about *you* change. This was Alex's experience. She said, "My parents aren't walking around me on tiptoes like they used to. Things are easier." Easier means more connected, less stressful, even happier. You can be more successful at home when you take responsibility for *yourself.*

When Things Go Wrong

In some families there is serious dysfunction and harm. Children are physically, emotionally, and sexually abused by parents and siblings. A father and mother may hurt each other. Someone in the family may be or become an alcoholic, or a drug addict, or commit a crime. The most important thing to do if something like this is going on in your family is to *seek help* right away. Too often I've seen family members cover up the dysfunction or abuse and pretend everything's OK. Maybe they're embarrassed or shameful or afraid they are going to get the person doing the harm in trouble. They present a mask to the outside world as if to prove, "We're fine!" But it's not fine. Something is seriously wrong.

If someone in your family is in trouble—whether it's you or a sibling or a parent—you must get help. You can't handle these situations alone because they are extreme and dangerous to everyone's mental, physical, and emotional help. If you don't get help you actually make matters much worse.

Maybe something really serious is happening with you and you've been trying to hide it, like being pregnant, or getting involved with drugs or crime, or you have become so depressed that you are thinking about taking your own life.

Know this: nothing is so horrible that it can't be helped. No matter how much you may feel like no one understands you, or that no one can help you, someone is there to help. I know this from deep personal experience. When I was in the depths of despair, part of my desperation was that I felt so bad I convinced myself I was beyond help. But I was wrong. Once I opened myself up to it, and told people who cared about me what was going on with me, I got the help I needed and I came through the difficult passage.

If you or someone in your family is in serious trouble there are many resources for you to draw on. Start with someone you can trust: a relative in your extended family; or a counselor; a teacher; a school nurse; a priest or a rabbi. They should be able to guide you to next steps. By asking for help you are doing the right thing, as painful as it may be to talk about what's going on. This is *especially* true if someone has threatened you if you *do* talk. This is an immediate and serious red flag and you have to treat it as such. At the end of this book is a list of web-based resources for you to use.

A home should be your safe harbor. What happens at home can affect the rest of your life right now and in the future. There are tensions and stresses in every family. They are not going to go away, and as you learn to deal with them in a calm, confident, and focused way you'll see how much better things can get for you and everyone else.

But I would be irresponsible if I didn't say that some homes are not safe. If yours is that way for you, you must seek help.

The Current of Love

Families are complex organisms. Just as you are growing and developing, so is your family. At one point in your life you may be very close to one or both parents, or your middle sister, or your little brother. And then, things shift, you grow apart. Maybe you become distant.

I hope, for everyone reading this book, that the deep current of love—between parent and child, between sisters and brothers—which is actually always there even if it is hidden or seems to have disappeared, will open again at the right time, when it needs to.

Remember: even though everything in life shifts, you can keep returning to the love you once felt for your family, even if it was only when you were a little child. That can guide you back to your heart. And to theirs.

CHAPTER 10

Comfortable Socially

Recently, I asked a group of teens ages thirteen through eighteen, "What are your biggest challenges socially?" Here's what they said:

- "Sometimes I don't want to do what my friends are doing."

- "Kids bully me. I'm scared."

- "I'm not into Facebook. Other kids think I'm weird."

- "I feel pressured to have sex."

- "I think people are smarter than I am so I don't speak up."

- "Other kids are better looking than me."

- "Sometimes I just don't feel like being with anybody else."

- "I was born in another country. I don't fit in here."

- "My family doesn't have money. I can't do stuff other kids do."

Can you see the common thread? The biggest challenge socially is feeling like you *fit in*.

Being comfortable socially means that when you're with your peers you enjoy being with them. You feel like you belong, like you're an equal, and that you are adding something to your relationships. In other words, you don't feel *un*comfortable. You don't feel weird or tense or anxious or want to run away.

Your social world, like school (chapter eight) and home (chapter nine), is one of the three major areas in your life. You want to succeed socially for a couple of reasons. First, you are with other kids a lot—in school, in extracurricular activities, in community clubs, in church, synagogue, or temple. So if you feel uncomfortable with your peers it's going to show up in many places and take up lots of your emotional energy.

Next, the social sphere is a major step out of the nest (your home and family) and into the world. Once you've finished high school you'll likely be on your own, even if you are still living at home. You'll be interacting with many different people. If you learn how to be successful socially as a teenager you are paving the way for that success as an adult.

Notice that I haven't said that being successful socially means you have to be "popular," or "good looking," a "great dresser," "super smart," have a "cool car," or any of that outward stuff. It means, quite simply, that you feel OK about yourself when you are with others. You are comfortable socially.

Unfortunately, for many teens, this is not the case. Since this is a time of major growth in your life—physically, mentally, emotionally, and spiritually—it is also the time for inner turmoil. One day you feel OK about yourself, the next day you don't. One morning you like the way you look, but by the afternoon you're a mess. One minute you believe people really like you, and the next minute you're sure they could care less. What you may not realize is that everyone else your age is feeling the same way about themselves as you are. The problem is that people generally don't want to talk about what's going on inside of them. They're afraid if they do, other people will *really* think they're weird, or people won't like them, or that they actually *are* weird. As we saw in chapter six, on confidence, keeping all of this inside of you produces major stress because you are disconnecting from the better, likable, OK parts of yourself. You're also disconnecting from everyone around you. Remember: disconnection causes stress.

In this chapter we're going to look at what it means to be better connected to others by being better connected to yourself. We'll do this by putting our attention on three different types of social situations: friendships, groups, and community. My aim is to show you how to use your growing awareness and the nine tools for being calm, confident, and focused so that you can cultivate productive habits in this key area of your life.

Friendships

One-on-one friendships can be nourishing, supportive, and joyous. Note, I said they "can be." They can also be frustrating, maddening, and heartbreaking. They can take up a lot of your time that you need to be spending on other things (like homework) or with other people (like your family). Some teens shy away from friendships because they find friends too demanding, or they've been hurt and they're afraid of being hurt again.

"Friendship" is a word that spans several types of relationships. Facebook diluted the word by using it to include anyone who has your name on their list and vice versa. According to my home page, I have hundreds of friends, but if I were to meet many of them tomorrow I wouldn't know what to say because I have no idea of who they are and vice versa. I think real friendships are something quite different than racking up names on a list. Friendship implies a connection where there is give-and-take of varying depth, intensity, and duration. It encompasses casual relationships, like the people you say "Hi" to as you pass them in the hall at school, to people you get together with occasionally, to your best friend, or your girlfriend or your boyfriend. The guidelines I'm going to give you here apply to any type of friendship.

The Challenge: Wanting to Be Liked

We all want other people to accept and like us. This is natural. But some teens, in order to gain friendship, end up doing things that they really don't want to do or wish they hadn't done. This includes "going along" with what someone else wants to do, whether it's a particular activity that you really aren't into, like seeing a certain movie, to things that may result in physical or emotional risk, like sex, to illegal activity, like using alcohol or drugs, shoplifting, or scrawling graffiti on public property.

A different way that people seek acceptance is by "showing off." They do daring things like speeding in cars and spending lots of money they don't really have. When people use these two ways of gaining friends—submission or bravado— it usually comes from not feeling good about themselves. So there are two unproductive habits at play: you keep acting in ways just to get people to like or accept you; and, more fundamentally, this is driven by an unproductive habit of not liking yourself. When you feel OK about yourself, you don't have to make yourself anything less or more than what you are.

The Solution: First, Like Yourself

One of the great challenges of your teenage years is accepting and liking yourself, having confidence in who you are. Do you remember the story I told in the first chapter about how much I did not like myself as a teenager? I was sure other people thought I looked strange, I was certain they felt I was too brainy and conscientious, and that I wasn't masculine enough. Reread that last sentence and see if you get a clue with what was *really* making me upset. It was my *idea* that I knew what *other people* were thinking about me. In psychology we call this "projection," which means you are projecting your thoughts into the other person and believe that's what *they* are thinking. That's how we convince ourselves that we are right. You say, *I know that other people think I'm a loser so I must be a loser*. What's really going on is that *you* think you're a loser. In my case I didn't like how I looked, I was shy about being smart, and I was comparing myself negatively to the guys on the football team. In other words: I wasn't accepting who I was. I projected my negative thinking about myself onto other kids. I was sure that *they* were thinking negatively about *me*. I remember being very surprised, if not shocked, when other kids told me how much they really liked me. Me? No way. What's the lesson here? If you don't like yourself, you may be just as surprised as I was to find out that your projections are wrong.

Many teens are fine with who they are. Sure, they'd like to be a little taller, or have different color hair or straighter teeth, but basically, they accept themselves. Yet a lot of teens don't like who they are. If that includes you then this is the time to shift your viewpoint about yourself. I'm saying this because I know, from personal and professional experience, that when you don't like yourself and you don't deal with it directly, you start doing all kinds of things to make yourself feel better—drinking, drugs, sex, excessive video games, shopping—or you'll shut down and withdraw. In either case you'll likely get depressed and want to give up. I did and it wasn't pretty. It took years to untangle the tight knot of self-loathing that I had tied myself into. Remember, the unproductive habit was my *belief* that I wasn't good enough. I kept repeating this until I was sure of it and projected that thought into others. I put myself in a losing situation. I couldn't see past the negative thinking and projections to see who I really was.

Let's pause for a moment to do the following exercise:

Exercise: Who You Really Are

- Sit comfortably in a chair with your back straight, and close your eyes.

- Breathe out three times. See the numbers 3, then 2, and then see the 1, big and bright and bold, facing you and reflecting you.

- See what you look like when you're not feeling good about yourself. What are you thinking? What do you look like? Breathe out.

- Now, turn to your right and look into a mirror where you see the image of your brightest and highest self: you at your best.

- What does that image look and feel like? Describe it to yourself.

- Now, the image in the mirror gives you a message. It tells you something about yourself that is good and true. What does it say?

- Open your eyes.

Frequent responses from the mirror are, "You're fine," "You're really great," "You're a good person." Over and over I've seen how many teens are so focused on the things they think are wrong about themselves; they can't see anything that's truly good. This unproductive habit ends up with them feeling down in the dumps, doing something self-destructive, and sometimes ready to give up.

The productive habit is to start accessing the ever-present positive side that each of us has. Imagine that there are two doors in front of you—on your left is the door that opens to a dark room where you're negative about yourself, and on your right is a door that leads to a room that's light-filled where you feel good about yourself. For all kinds of reasons—culturally and personally—we are in the unproductive habit of consistently veering left and ending up in a dark place: "Life sucks, and my life *really* sucks." We need to make a different choice and start steering ourselves in the direction of the light: to what is right and good about ourselves. If you do the exercise consistently on a daily basis, you will be building this productive habit, and you'll notice that your attention starts to shift more readily, and naturally, to your positive side. Remember, the negative side goes nowhere. It's like having your phone ring every day with the same robo-recording message that says, "Hello, you're a loser." Hang up on that caller! Disconnect that phone. Get a new number.

It may seem obvious, but if you don't accept yourself you are at war with yourself and you will end up defeated. Why? Because *you can't be anyone else than who you are.* Have you ever heard the expression, "You might as well be who you are. Everyone else is taken"? It's true.

Using the Confidence Tools

I'm sure you realized by now that liking yourself is what we were covering in chapter seven on Confidence. Confidence means having faith in yourself, being loyal to who you are. When you don't have confidence in yourself it's almost impossible to succeed in your social world because you're setting yourself up for failure. I'm not saying that you have to start bragging or thinking you're the best thing since the latest version of Xbox. I'm talking about you being OK with who you are and I'm showing you how to put the Confidence tools, particularly *confide* and *reflect,* into action.

The point here is that you will bring whatever feelings you have about yourself into your social relationships. So first do a little "housecleaning" so that you can bring your best self into any friendship or social connection. Spend a few minutes considering the following question. What three to five positive qualities do you have to bring to a friendship? Lists often include these qualities: "I care about my friends"; "I'm generous"; "I have a good sense of humor"; and "I'm considerate."

Make your list now. Once you've made it, and you're aligned with your best self, let's look at the qualities that are the foundation of a good friendship.

What Are the Qualities of a Good Friendship?

Honesty. A good friendship is secure on a bedrock of honesty. If one of you lies or stretches the truth you will damage the trust necessary for a good, possibly long-lasting friendship. You'll hurt the other person and ultimately yourself. When you lie you always carry around the aching feeling that you haven't told the truth and you have to keep making up stories to cover your tracks. Mark Twain, the great American author, once quipped, "When you tell the truth you never have to remember anything."

Tell the truth.

There are two situations in a friendship when telling the truth is challenging: when you see your friend doing something hurtful to themselves or others, and when one of you is hurt by something the other has done. Let's look at these.

When a friend is hurting themselves or someone else. Jason, a fifteen-year-old I know, watched his friend Drew hurt himself and others. Jason explained, "Drew kept having trouble with girlfriends. He'd start off with a girl and things would be cool and then they would go bad. Girls didn't want to go out with him after the first or second date. Drew didn't know why. I could tell Drew was putting these girls down, not in obvious ways, but he said things like, 'Wow, you'd really look good in a different color.' I know that doesn't sound too bad, but Drew commented on almost everything a girl said, or did, or thought. The comments always sounded to the girls like Drew was constantly correcting or criticizing them. It added up. No one wants to hang out with that kind of criticism."

I asked Jason what he said to Drew when he saw this going on. "One day when we were hanging out, I asked Drew if he knew why girls were dumping him. He said, 'I guess they don't like me,' but he didn't really have a good idea of why that was. I was honest and told him what I saw." I appreciated Jason for being honest with Drew, and then asked him why he thought one of the girls didn't tell Drew directly. Jason thought for a moment and said, "It's really hard to be truthful; you don't want to hurt the other person."

Often I coach people who are in friendships or close relationships who have this difficulty. They don't want to tell the truth but end up being hurt themselves, as these girls were. What do you do in this situation? It's simple: always make a statement that starts with "I" rather than one that starts with "you". A girl dating Drew who didn't like his critical remarks could say, "I feel criticized when you make comments like that. I feel hurt that you don't like me just the way I am." This is very different than if she said, "You're so critical! You say hurtful things. Stop being a jerk. Cut it out!" People are able to hear "I" statements much more easily because they don't feel attacked.

When you make an "I" statement you are loyal to yourself. You are honest about what *you* are feeling or thinking. If your friend cares about you and your friendship they won't want to keep hurting you. Have confidence in your own experience. Bring that confident self into a friendship. Though it may be challenging when you hit rough spots in your friendship together, the relationship will be so much the better for it, and so will you.

And what if you've done something that hurt your friend? Admit your error as soon as possible. Say, "I'm sorry for what I did to you. I didn't mean to hurt you. I won't do it again." Simple. Tell the truth. Zoë did this when she hurt her friend Cheryl. They had planned to get together to work on a class project, and then, at the last moment, Zoë got invited to a concert and forgot all about her plan to work with Cheryl. As soon as she realized her mistake Zoë called Cheryl and apologized. While this didn't completely resolve the situation—Zoë then needed to ask the teacher for an extension on the project—Zoë showed her friend that she made a mistake, was sorry her friend was hurt, and she was prepared to fix the situation as best she could.

In both situations I've just described the people were using the Focus tools. If a goal of a good friendship is honesty, when you see you are being distracted from that goal by not telling the truth . . . Stop! Ask yourself, "Is my dishonesty helping me to reach my goal?" The answer will be "no." Now listen to your inner voice giving you specific guidance. Likely it will be "tell the truth." Now see yourself fulfilling the direction of the voice: be honest with your friend by using an "I" statement. Get back on track with your goal. If your friend doesn't really want you to be honest, you need to seriously evaluate if this is a friendship you want to have in your life.

Mutuality. In a good friendship both people share each other's attention. It isn't lopsided, as it was for Katie. Katie was such a good listener that all her friends used her shoulders to cry on. But no one listened to her. Katie's constant attention to her friends was actually a cover for her secret feeling that she wasn't important enough to deserve *their* attention. When she accepted that she too had difficult things in her life that she also needed to talk about and share, her friendships started changing. There was more give-and-take. She could see that other kids really liked her. But this was only after she started respecting and liking herself. Mutuality means that each person makes equal demands on the relationship in terms of time, interest, and emotion. If you feel like a friendship is draining you, it's missing mutuality.

Individuality. While it may seem paradoxical, given what I just said about mutuality, a good friendship is between individuals. This means that to be friends you don't have to like the same things or think the same way. Maybe you do sometimes and maybe you don't. You may have a different point of view on all kinds of subjects, from food, to school, to politics, to sex. Neither one of you has to be right. Think about what you give to each other and what you can learn from one another, what each of you offers the relationship as an individual in your own right. Individuality in a friendship teaches you how to respect each others' outlook, opinion, and taste.

Don't try to make everyone be just like you. It won't work. That's conformity, and sooner or later one of you is going to get tired of the friendship. Here's where the Confidence tools come in: if you are feeling negatively about yourself, then correct it by going to the mirror, confiding in your highest self, and receiving the reflection of what is accurate and positive about you. Then you are operating from a position of wholeness, where real mutuality is possible.

Clarifying Expectations. In any friendship ask yourself, "What do I expect from this person? Is it reasonable?" I think it's reasonable to expect honesty, mutuality, and individuality in a friendship, and I'm encouraging you to think along the same lines. So many things fall under these categories we've just discussed.

Take this situation between Marcy and her friend Jayne. Marcy complained to me one day, "Jayne is texting me, all the time! I really like her a lot and we're good friends but sometimes I feel like yelling 'Stop!'" What was going on here? Marcy and Jayne had different expectations for the friendship. Jayne wanted a friend to be available at all times and Marcy needed some space. I encouraged Marcy to share this with Jayne: to be honest, and come from a place of mutuality and individuality. After they had a discussion Marcy reported back, "I told her that I liked her and our friendship, but that I have a lot of other things going on and getting so many texts from her is hard for me because I need to get my work done." Notice Marcy's "I" statements. Jayne was able to hear them and made the necessary adjustments for the friendship to continue. I recommend discussing expectations early on in a friendship when there's a sign that you both might have different expectations of each other. That way, hidden resentments don't build which could disturb or end the friendship later on.

Keep Your Promises. If you promise something to a friend, keep your word. A promise is an agreement. If you break agreements, it fractures trust. A good friendship is built on trust. Promises come in different shapes and sizes. You and your friend decide that you'll meet at four o'clock in the afternoon and go to the gym together. Four o'clock rolls around and your friend is nowhere to be seen. You text him. He replies, "Dang. I forgot." An agreement, a promise, is broken. Or you tell someone something personal and ask them to promise not to tell anyone else. They break the promise, and your trust, when they end up spilling the beans to someone else. Friends have to be able to trust each other. Without trust there is suspicion, fear, and withholding. This does not mean you have to tell each other everything all the time. You don't. But if you promise not to share what your friend has told you and then you do, you've been dishonest and broken your friend's trust. If you've made a promise that you later think you're going to have trouble keeping, you first need to talk with the person you've made the promise with. Don't make a mess and then have to clean it up.

Supporting Each Other. Good friends support one another. When things get rough at home or at school for one of you, you know the other person is there to talk with and give you support. What does "giving support" actually mean? Do you remember, in chapter six on confidence (and earlier in this chapter in the exercise on page 153), the mirror that you confided in? A good friend is like that mirror. You can reflect back to each other what you really see, especially the other person's good qualities. We need that because sometimes we are highly critical about ourselves and tend to see only the bad stuff.

A good friend is also like a mirror in being non-judgmental and non-critical. The mirror simply reflects. It is only in the fairy tale *Snow White and the Seven Dwarves* that the mirror says what characters want them to. Mirrors accurately reflect back your positive qualities. They can also show you your negative ones. Your friend is your mirror—your confidant. Someone you can trust to tell it like it is without any agenda of hurting you or being better than you. In fact, it's quite the opposite. A good friend cares about you, just like you do about them.

Use the Focus Tools. All of the qualities of a good friendship—honesty, mutuality, trust—must start with you. To be a good friend you need to have a goal of being a good friend to yourself first. If you have the goal of being honest with yourself, and the goal of keeping your promises to yourself, then do that. Stay focused. If you get distracted and start taking actions away from these goals you'll break your promises and do to yourself what you wouldn't tolerate from a friend.

Topher provided a good example. His goal was to lose weight, but he couldn't stay away from that extra bowl of ice cream. "I know I shouldn't do it, but it's like, the ice cream tub is calling out my name. I just give in." Topher and I worked on how he could use the Focus tools to stay on track with his goal of losing weight (and thereby feeling better about himself). When he came back for his next coaching session he had a big smile and said, "You'll be proud of me, Dr. B. Last night I finished a bowl of ice cream and I started dipping the scoop back into the container for more, and I did what you said, I used the Focus tools. I stopped. Then I asked myself, 'Is taking another scoop leading me to my goal of losing weight?' Of course the answer was 'no!', so then I listened to my inner radio station. It said, 'Put a lid on it,' and I did, literally. I closed the tub of ice cream and put it back in the freezer."

If Topher was supporting a friend who stayed on track like this he'd say to the friend, "Good going! Congratulations!" And that's exactly what I said to him. Not only did he feel better about himself from having accomplished his goal, but this better feeling resulted in making easier friendships. When you like who you are, you enjoy being with people, and they enjoy being with you. Notice, I said, "Like who you are." I did not say, "When you are in love with yourself." People usually don't find that very attractive.

The take-away here is this: be a good friend to yourself. The next natural step will be making good friends with others.

Groups

There are many different types of groups in school and out. I'm not talking about "groupings" (the people in your history class). I mean named groups: the football team, the debating society, the computer club. I also mean the cliques of people who seem to more naturally relate to each other and thus become groups of their own.

The extracurricular groups (sports, common interest, etc.) are structured by way of *activity* and *purpose*. Everybody who's in the group is there to participate in a specific, common endeavor, from stamp collection to lacrosse, with the goal of advancing knowledge or a skill set. Common interest groups can be fun and demanding. One student I was coaching joined the crew team in her junior year and was up and on the water at six o'clock every morning, five days a week. These activity groups can be very rewarding: sharing a passionate purpose, working as a team, and each person making his or her individual contribution.

If you are a member of a group, here is the vital question: are you there because *you* want to be or because someone said you should? I understand that you need to build your resumé for your college and job applications, but you are wasting your time and draining the group's energy if you are less than enthusiastic about being part of the group's endeavor. This is a Focus issue. What is your goal and does it line up with the goal of the group?

To be a good group member, you need to be dedicated and hold up your end since the group is a team of people. In other words, as a member, you are a part of something bigger. But, if you're in a group and you really don't want to be there, you are going to cause stress for yourself and others. In other words, you are disconnecting; and as we know, disconnection is the major cause of stress. The bottom line is this: you can't be a part *of* and *apart from* at the same time. Choose one or the other.

If you're in a group and you're not fully engaged most of the time, if you're not enjoying the work of the group or the people in it, it's probably not the right group for you. You have to be honest about this with yourself. You might feel that you're not "good enough" for the group (you think the other kids are, take your pick: smarter, more talented, better able to focus, etc.) There may be things about the way the group is organized or about one or more of its members that you don't like. Talk these things over with a friend, a parent, your school guidance counselor, or an older sibling (if you have one). While you may be able to affect some changes in the group once you've become involved and people see you are a committed group member, it's unreasonable to expect that you're going to like everything that everyone does in the group all the time. That said, if your experience is going too much in the negative direction you're only hurting yourself and others by grudgingly staying involved.

Erica faced this situation with the cheerleading team in her high school. It was a big status point to be accepted on the squad and Erica had the goal of getting a place since she was in middle school and watched her older sister Grace serve as its captain. Erica did everything she could to get herself ready for the tryouts: she practiced the moves over and over until she could do them all with ease and she won a coveted spot. A month into the season, though, she was having second thoughts, "I didn't really like how the girls made themselves out to be better than everyone else." She disliked the way they often dissed other girls, and sometimes the gossip was about personal friends of hers who weren't cheerleaders. When Erica told her mom she was ready to quit the squad, her mother suggested Erica talk with the coach. The coach told Erica that other girls were also uncomfortable with the gossiping, and the coach called a team meeting. The group talked it over and decided that gossiping was off-limits, and, by group consensus, if it went on it would result in suspension from the squad.

Erica's story brings up two important points: (1) you are a member of a group and as a group member you have something to add. You don't have to go against your own principles and go along with everyone else in order to be liked. Use the Focus tools. If you find yourself doing something that doesn't agree with your own principles, Stop! Listen, and Fulfill. Follow your inner compass about what's right to do. (2) Gossip is always toxic. I say that because it's motive is inevitably to put someone else down, be better than them, or deflect attention away from the person who is instigating the gossiping (what is *their* motive?). Gossip breeds trouble. It is inconsistent with all of the principles of good relationships covered earlier in this chapter: honesty, mutuality, and individuality. If you don't like something someone else is doing, talk to them directly, or talk with someone (like a teacher, coach or parent) who can help facilitate an intervention.

Always remember your goal to have and maintain honest, trusting relationships. Take actions that keep you focused on the goal: being direct and telling the truth. Gossiping is a distraction because it will lead you into a pit of negativity.

Community

I'm tempted to begin this section with one of the few "shoulds" in this book. I usually steer clear of saying you "should" do anything because it's a quick way of getting people—especially teens—to resist. "Why *should* I?" is the expected and natural response to being told what you should do. So, here's the "should," followed by the reason: *you should get involved in your community.* Why? Because a community gives you the opportunity to act in ways that benefit others, and that's a direct route to personal fulfillment and success.

How do I know this? Because it's based on truth: we humans are social animals and we depend on one another for our very existence. Each of us is part of something larger: the family to which we belong, the school we attend, the teams we play on, the houses of worship where we pray, the communities in which we live, the towns, cities, states, and nations in which we are citizens, and the hemisphere, continent, and entire planet we inhabit. You and I and everyone are all players on Team Earth. Playing your part means giving of yourself for the greater good. When you contribute to your community (however you define that word), you are fulfilling your purpose as a member of that community. Each of us is part of the whole. Unfortunately, we tend to think about what we can *get* from the community, rather than what we can *give*.

So much of our culture is based on taking—or owning—for ourselves: more money, more objects, more status. This creates a deep chasm between the "haves" and the "have-nots." In a world in which fifteen million children die of starvation every year, you might conclude that there isn't enough to go around. In truth, it's quite the opposite! There *is* enough, in fact, there is plenty. But there is also such gross inequality in how resources are cultivated and distributed throughout the world, and such grotesque accumulation of wealth by so few people that the "have-nots" suffer greatly. Imagine: fifteen *million* children—people younger than you—who die of starvation *every single year*. That's almost twice the entire population of New York City. When you take a moment to grasp the stunning enormity of this and realize that in your own way you could play a part in creating a change, a shift, by giving of yourself, you will understand why I started this section off with "you should get involved with your community." *The health, and life, of your community and our world depends on you and your contribution.*

If you're thinking "Come on, Dr. B! Aren't you being a little *dramatic*?" the answer is "no." The reason I'm telling you to get involved in your community, like everything else in this book, is because I want you to know, now, what will make your life a success. I wish someone had given me this guidance when I was your age. Instead, I had to discover everything I've written about—including getting involved in my community—on my own. After being painfully isolated and insulated for many years, I realized this was a root cause of my unhappiness and dissatisfaction with life. Disconnection causes stress and unhappiness. When I started to turn this around, when I started truly giving to others, I gained so much.

While friendships and social group involvement depend on mutuality and give-and-take, community groups offer you a different opportunity: to give of yourself for the benefit of others. If you attend church, synagogue, mosque, or temple, your community of worshippers often share of themselves with the larger communities in which they live. For instance, my synagogue opens its doors to people who cannot afford our membership fee but are looking for a place to worship, to study scriptures, and find solace in communion with others and with the Divine.

Every community has its own groups: Boy Scouts, Girl Scouts, youth radio stations, old age homes, rescue missions for abused pets, and many others. Happily, the list is endless. And, if you identify a need in your community that isn't being fulfilled, that's an opportunity for you to find a way to fill that need. Start a community group. In the winter, friends of mine in Maine send out a squad of teenagers to shovel snow from the walkways and driveways of elderly people who would otherwise be homebound during a snowstorm because they don't have the strength, or the means, to do their own shoveling.

When you live just for yourself it is a one-dimensional existence. Flat. Sure, you take care of your own needs, but life is so much more than that. It includes—and needs—*other people*. Participating in community activities adds a necessary dimension to your life. You contribute to and serve a larger whole. If you're not already involved in a community-based activity I strongly encourage you to explore the opportunities and possibilities. Quite literally, they can change your life.

I strongly believe that as human beings we are truly fulfilled when we give to others. "Giving" means exactly that: offering what we can, of ourselves, to add to, better, or help shift someone else's life, without the motive of receiving anything in return. Our world, our country, our states, and local communities—your neighbors—may be crying out for help, and you, and every one of your friends or family members, can serve a purposeful role in making a contribution to their lives.

Recently I took on a part-time job at a public nursing home, a place where old people who are ill and have no resources can receive medical care and have a place to live until they die. These SNFs ("skilled nursing facilities") are often sad places: there is usually very little to do and social interaction is limited. It is a get-by existence.

My role as a psychologist was to go in each week and spend time with a handful of patients, talking about whatever they wanted to. I noticed by the third visit that their talk was filled with complaints—about the staff, the food, the smells, the doctors. While I may have served a useful function as a listener, it occurred to me that I might be able to offer something else, something more valuable and uplifting to these people. The nursing home was down the block from a public market. I asked each of the patients if, instead of sitting inside and talking, they might like to take a walk, or have me push their wheelchair, to the market so we could have a cup of coffee or tea together. To a person, everyone said, "Yes!" and every week I took each of them out for a little excursion to the market. On the way we stopped and looked at flowers and at the market we smiled at cute babies in strollers. The half hour that we were together had transformed from gloomy complaining to light-filled enjoyment.

I hope this story inspires you to consider what you can do to bring some relief or small pleasure to someone in your community. Maybe you can read a book to an old person in a nursing home, or play circle games with little kids at a local daycare center, or work in a pet-rescue mission, or organize a cleanup operation of an empty lot so others can play there or plant a community garden.

What does "community" mean? First, it's not a "thing." Rather it is a shared bond amongst people. And this bond doesn't just "happen"— it is the result of each member offering what he or she can to the greater good. We could say that community is more a "feeling" than it is a physical entity. And the feeling that generates from you and others giving of themselves is, in a word, love.

Years ago, my college roommate and his late wife, both ministers, opened a boat building workshop. They took in teenage boys who had messed up, or were having difficulties in getting along with others, or who were one step away from being put in prison, and trained them to be expert boat builders. The story of this boat shop is so extraordinary. My friend and his wife had no money or resources to start or maintain a boat shop, but over thirty-five years other people gave them everything they needed to fulfill this mission: tools, tractors, even barns and houses and land. Not only did they train the boys to have viable skills that would last them a lifetime, but each year they engaged the boys in many community activities, like shoveling snow that I mentioned earlier, or fixing someone's roof, or numerous other projects that helped people out. When the boys left the boat shop they took with them valuable trade skills of carpentry, but their hearts were opened and they took something even deeper and more long lasting: the experience of giving, of belonging.

No matter how busy your life is, no matter how much or how little you have or own, know that there are always people who can benefit from what you have to give.

Let's do a final exercise:

Exercise: What Can I Give?

- Sit comfortably in a chair with your back supported and your head resting on its pedestal.

- Breathe out anything that disturbs you or limits you.

- See any inner disturbance of limitation leave you on a thin veil of gray smoke.

- Now breathe out three times: see the numbers 3, 2, and then see the 1 big and bright and bold, facing you, reflecting you, tall and strong.

- Now see yourself standing in a circle of white light.

- With you in this circle are people you know and people you don't know.

- Sense and see and feel something that you have to offer these people.

- It can be something you care about, or feel passionate about, something that's important to you.

- See yourself sharing it with them, and see them receiving what you have to offer.

- See the circle of white light getting brighter as it clarifies and nourishes all of the people in the circle, including you.

- Breathe out and open your eyes.

As I close this chapter, let's take a moment to reflect on which leg of the stool we're working on here. If you're thinking "The Focus leg, of course!" you're right. Focus has to do with having a goal and taking actions that take you to the goal. When you can see that your goal, as a human being, as a member of the world community, is to contribute to making this a better place for everyone, it will be clear and natural for you to realize the way to make this happen is to give to your community. Remember, the productive habit is to join and contribute; the unproductive one is to close down and pull away.

Before you get out of bed each morning, with your eyes still closed, ask yourself this question: *What can I do today to make someone else's life happier, easier, better?*

What do you see yourself doing? Then open your eyes and see it with open eyes.

CHAPTER 11

DR. B's A to Z

In my work with people like you I've found that many teens want to know about the same things, especially what's going on inside of them and how to understand and deal with the sometimes crazy world around them. As I've said throughout this book, it's vital that you ask questions. In my experience, it's an essential part of your learning and growing process.

Since one book can't possibly answer all of your questions, I thought it might be helpful to offer my thoughts on some of the topics and issues that keep recurring. For this informal A to Z, I've selected three or four for each letter of the alphabet. I could have easily chosen ten or twenty per letter, so this is a culled, though not random, selection. As you will see, some entries are relatively short, some longer.

If, as you read through these entries, you feel I've omitted or missed something important, please send me an email to (teensguidetosuccess@ gmail.com). Your suggestions and questions are important to me; they tell me what you're dealing with and struggling with. They tell me what you want to know.

As you read each entry, ask yourself: "What do *I* think about this? Do I agree with Dr. B or not?" Discuss your thoughts with friends and family. Send me an email and share your thoughts with me. They will help guide my future writing and web postings.

After each entry there are suggestions as to what part of this book would be additionally helpful (in the order of their priority). If you want to learn more about anything I've mentioned here, or would like to read someone else's perspective, go online, do some research, look things up. For every item in this A to Z, there are literally hundreds of thousands of hits on the web. In the not-so-distant past, if you wanted to know about something you either owned an encyclopedia at home, or more likely, you had to leave your house and go to a library and search through stacks of books until you found what you were looking for. Now you can stretch out on your couch at home and find out about everything, immediately.

If you want more information about something here or you need more help with an issue you are struggling with, I strongly encourage you to seek out and get the help you need. As a rule of thumb, always start close to home: talk with your parent, guardian, brother, or sister. If you are dealing with a sensitive issue and feel you need someone with a little distance, talk with a teacher, a member of the clergy, or a counselor. The next circle out are online forums, chat rooms, phone-in information lines, and telephone hot lines. All you need to do is reach out for help and it is there. No matter how isolated you may feel, there are others who feel just like you do, and there are a great number of resources available to you right now.

Abuse

A person who abuses someone else is using a position of power or influence to take advantage of the other person, often forcing them to do something against their will. Abuse can be physical (beating), sexual (making someone do something sexually), financial (draining another person's resources), emotional (provoking fear), and online (spreading untrue stories and intimate details in a public way). Sadly, many adults abuse children, even their own. But abusers (called "perpetrators") can be any age. One child bullying another child is an abuser. The perpetrator often threatens the victim to be silent and never tell anyone. Abuse is a criminal act. It must be stopped immediately. If you are being abused, or you know someone who is the victim of abuse, find someone you trust and tell them. Let them help you to look after your safety and well-being.
See: Calm, Confident, Focus

Addictions

Addictions are long-term, ingrained, self-abusive, unproductive habits. They are always self-destructive and can involve any one or more of the following:

alcohol, drugs, sex, nicotine, shopping, or gambling. Addictions develop over time and often start from having feelings of isolation, anxiety, or depression. At the root of every addiction is an unfulfilled natural human need for connection, especially to something greater, often spiritual. If you are addicted, admit it to a parent, sibling, friend, teacher, counselor, or clergy. You cannot get rid of an addiction all alone (that's how you got into it). There are excellent, free resources available to you, like twelve-step groups. Take action now.
See: Calm, Confidence, Focus

Anger

Anger often gets sparked when you expect something to happen in a certain way and it doesn't. You expect a call from your boyfriend and he spaces out. You expect the teacher will summarize how to prepare for the final and she doesn't. You expect that your parents will raise your allowance and they don't. The next time you're angry at someone or about something ask yourself this question, "What was I just expecting that didn't happen the way I expected?" The world doesn't always work the way we would like it to. Your anger won't change a situation that's already past, and staying angry doesn't do anyone any good. What went wrong? What did you learn from it? Get it, move on, and do it differently the next time.
See: Calm, Focus

Appreciation

Appreciating someone is one of the best medicines you can give to a relationship. Appreciation means you see the value the other person adds to your life, and you express your gratitude to them. Cultivate a practice of appreciating one person every day ("I appreciate how you cook dinner every night, Mom!") and watch them light up and see your relationship get better; it won't happen instantly, but it builds as you keep finding things to appreciate. Also, appreciate yourself once a day ("I really studied well"). For some people this is a lot more challenging than appreciating someone else. That's because many of us live in a state of negativity. Try appreciations. Guidelines: be specific, and sincere. Mean what you say and feel it.
See: Focus, Confidence

Bedtime

Get to bed at a reasonable hour. Too many teens are sleep deprived. A common excuse is "too much homework," which is often a cover for giving into distractions (texting, Facebook, surfing the web, television, etc.). Imagine yourself, the next day, as the teacher facing twenty or more bleary-eyed, sleep deprived students just like you. Not fun. Another good rule of thumb is to stop working on the computer an hour before you get into bed. One of my brothers, who had sleep problems for years, actually does this and he finds it remarkably effective.
See: Focus

Beliefs

Beliefs are something you hold as true ("God exists"). Everyone has a different belief system. Don't make other people wrong if they believe something different than you. Then your belief becomes a prejudice. Make sure what you believe in is for your highest purpose and for humankind as well. Beliefs can be helpful in times of turmoil and chaos to give you a steady anchor. Beliefs can also refer to the trust and faith you have in yourself ("I believe in my possibilities").
See: Confidence, Focus

Body Image

Many people tend to perceive their own body (their "body image") differently than others perceive them. Someone who is anorexic (a person who starves herself to maintain an unhealthy thinness) is afraid she'll look fat if she eats anything. We tend to be much more critical of our bodies and than others are ("My nose is so big! Ugh"). In addition to anorexia, distortions in body image can also result in bulimia (purging); both are dangerous. These conditions need immediate counseling and intervention. Your body is your home for life. Get to know it, respect it, and like it. If you're not happy with your body image, do something healthy to develop it.

Competition

Competition should bring out the best in you. Life is not a competition with anyone else but yourself. Become the best person *you* can be. If you "win"

or "lose" at something make sure you learn from what you did or didn't do. Otherwise, winning or losing will only temporarily pump up or deflate your ego (see "Ego" below). Competition, in its most negative form, is often the root cause of bullying: using abuse and force to be "better than."
See: Confidence

Creativity

Everyone has it and everyone expresses it differently, whether it's by baking a cake, building a boat, playing the piano, or singing with your little brother. It is tied into your imagination, which is a very active force and can lead to creative acts large and small. Your creativity is the "voice" inside of you. When you consistently tune into it, it will guide you.

Criticism

Criticism helps when it is a truth that prompts you to do things better next time. It can hurt when it's not delivered with that intent. When someone criticizes you and it's hard for you to hear, ask yourself, "What's hard about this?" Is it the person's manner or are they saying something true that you don't want to hear? Be grateful for criticism that's meant to help you. If you criticize someone else make sure you're clear on your intent. Is it to "top dog" yourself, or is it because you want to offer the other person something that could genuinely help them? Make sure it's coming from the right place, a place of caring and love.

Dating

Dating can be fun. It can also take up a lot of your time, emotional energy, and money. Determine together some boundaries that will work for each of you about how much time you'll spend together and when. You each have a whole life going on and dating is just one part of it.
See: Will, Calm, Confidence, and Focus

Discipline

Discipline has negative connotations for most people. That's too bad because the most successful people are very disciplined. Think of discipline as a corral

for a wild horse. The horse has tremendous, unbounded energy. The corral keeps it bounded so the horse's energy can be used effectively. When you have discipline in how you manage your resources—your health (what you eat, when you exercise), your time, and your money—you can actually create a lot possibilities for yourself. Every spiritual tradition teaches the value in discipline.
See: Focus

Drama

Many teens—and adults—create a lot of drama in their lives. Daily drama is often a distraction from what needs to be taken care of, whether it's homework or a challenging relationship. Sometimes creating drama in your life (and with those around you) is an addiction in itself: you can only deal with things if it's all very *dramatic*. Leave the drama for the theater or the movies. Your life is not a soap opera; don't make it into one.
See: Chapter thirteen

Eating

Your body and brain are growing. Give them what they need to be healthy. Ice cream, Coke, pizza? If you have to, but in moderation. When your diet is principally made up of things that are not good for you, you're bound to do other things that are not good for you. You are what you eat. If you have a problem with obesity, or a food addiction, or an eating disorder like anorexia or bulimia, get professional help. Don't endanger your health. When you eat, eat slowly, chew the food. Taste it. Be grateful for it.
See: Focus, Calm

Ego

Usually used to describe people who are filled with an inflated sense of self as in, "She's got a big ego." Spiritual traditions see this "big ego" as the cause of human suffering. You think you're controlling everything and when things don't happen your way you're hurt, angry, or doubtful. That's your ego. When you stop trying to make the world in your image and simply cultivate the best in yourself so you can bring out the best in others, then your ego is in check.
See: Focus

Environment

There are two environments: outer and inner. Keep your inner environment in good shape with healthy food, regular exercise, and using your mind in productive ways. When you do that you'll be in a better position to contribute to the outer environment, which is the one we all share. In twenty to thirty years you and your peers will be running this world. It drives me crazy to see teens carelessly toss empty Snickers wrappers and other garbage on the street. The world is not your bedroom. It is in your hands.

See: Chapter thirteen

Fantasy

Fantasy is a way of using your imagination to dream up things that have no basis in reality and are impossible or improbable. Sometimes these are about another person we dream about having a relationship with. Fantasies can be sexual in nature. If you dwell on the same fantasy it's best to look at what's really going on: What do you want that you don't or can't have? What do you feel is missing in your life? A fantasy doesn't mean you have to act on it, yet it can provide you with some useful information about yourself.

See: Focus

Fear

Fear is usually about something specific (snakes, heights, flying, driving over a bridge). It can grow into anxiety, which is an overall feeling of tension and dread. Anxiety can be connected with guilt about something you did in the past (see "Guilt" below) or about its consequences. Fear and anxiety can disturb your sleep, your ability to digest food, and can drive your blood pressure up above normal levels.

Use all nine tools: Calm, Confidence, and Focus.

Fun

Have fun when you can; we all need to laugh and play regularly. Never have fun at someone else's expense and always make sure your fun is legal. If you are determined to have fun by experimenting with drugs or sex, it's best that you discuss your plan with an adult first, preferably a parent. Remember: what's fun for someone else may be a nightmare for you and vice versa. You can always say "no," to someone else's fun.

See: Focus, Calm

Grounded

When you're in the present we say you're grounded, like earth and roots. It suggests stability. When your mind is flipping from the past or future, or you are unrealistic, you are out in space somewhere and we say you're ungrounded. Get back into the present by using the Calm tools. "Grounded" is also used by parents as a punishment (you have to stay in your room). Unfortunately, it gives the word negative connotations.

See: Calm

Government

Like the environment, there are two types: inner and outer. How you govern yourself means how you run your life. Do you have standards for yourself? Do you live by them? Do you see what happens when you fall short and do you correct the issue? The "outer government" is the system of laws and moral codes that we live by. You have a voice and a vote in both. Use them.

See: Chapter thirteen

Guilt

In court, a person is found guilty when the judge or jury determines they were responsible for the crime. When you feel guilty it's because you did something and you are not taking responsibility for it. Guilt is a lingering sense of incompletion, sometimes but not always attached to a wrong doing. When we feel guilty we are keeping ourselves stuck in the past. If you did something you feel is wrong, admit it. The next step is moving on. Guilt keeps you stuck in the past. Now you're in the present.

Happiness

Happiness is often thought to depend on externals like other people or objects; if you have the object, or have more of it, then you'll be happy. But inevitably whatever it is that's "making you happy" will die, go away, or you will lose

it. Spiritual traditions teach that real happiness is not dependent on anything outside yourself, but comes from a deep inner sense of being part of something much, much larger than yourself, whether you call that God or Higher Power or Inner Self. As you cultivate that connection you'll be happier.
See: Focus

Health

Your health is your responsibility. When you were a baby you were helpless; your health was totally dependent on your parents. Now it depends on the choices you make every day. Health doesn't just mean a strong body. There's mental health (your thoughts), emotional health (your feelings), and spiritual health (your connection to something larger). Observe yourself for a week: what are you doing on a daily basis to keep yourself healthy in your body, mind, and spirit?

Hormones

Hormones are chemicals produced inside your body to stimulate its growth. In puberty—the strange name given to the time when your body starts to change—growth is triggered in both boys and girls by increased levels of the sex hormone testosterone. This chemical also triggers the sexual organs to develop. Hormones can bring on mood swings, feeling uncomfortable in your body and being emotionally sensitive. Have you ever heard the phrase "raging hormones"? That could be you right now.
See: Puberty, Calm

Imagination

Your imagination produces creative ideas, solutions to problems, fantasies, and dreams. Your imagination is working all the time, when you are sleeping and when you are wide awake. It can tell you valuable things about yourself, what you're dealing with at any particular moment, or give you a clue on how to handle something. Use your imagination when you're studying for a test to boost your confidence and your ability to focus.
See: Confidence, Focus

Integrity

Integrity means being honest and having moral principles ("Jim acted with integrity in that difficult situation") and being whole and undivided ("Rosa is really integrated as a person"). When you are calm, confident, and focused you are in that state of wholeness, which naturally goes along with being good for your word.

See: Focus, Chapter thirteen

Internet

The Internet is an amazing resource and now part of the daily fabric of our lives. It should be used to bring people together to create and sustain a better world, not just to let people know who you were with last night or what band you like. It can eat up a lot of your time, energy, and money and can become an addiction). Be careful and wise with how you spend your time online.

See: Addiction, Focus

Jobs

Get one. Making some money is a good thing when you're a teenager. You'll learn about responsibility, commitment, contribution, and relating to people who are not your family or friends.

See: Focus, Confidence

Jittery

Ever notice your legs bobbing up and down compulsively? Or your eyes jumping around, or your mind flitting from one scene to another? "Jittery" is a synonym for "nervous," a sign of being unable to calm down and relax. If you notice one of those signs, use the Calm tools.

See: Calm

Judgmental

You're judgmental when you have or display an excessively critical point of view. "Jen's makeup today is, like . . . eeeeuuuu." "Max is stupid." "Maggie is too smart for her own good." When you're passing judgment on someone or

something, you are determining that's the way it is because *you said so*. You're the judge and the jury. Being judgmental gets in the way of seeing things as they are, appreciating the different sides of a person or idea, of taking someone else's point of view, of having a more balanced outlook. Often we become judgmental when someone acts in a way that triggers something we don't like in ourselves. If you're feeling judgmental about someone or something see if you can take three steps back and look at what's really going on with *you*.
See: Focus

Knowledge

Real knowing comes from being active in the world, not by memorizing facts out of books. The ancient Greek dictum, "Know Thyself," is necessary for right living. Know who *you* are. What are *your* likes, dislikes, limitations, and possibilities? Seek to know, to really learn, the subject you are studying in school. Memorizing bits of information just to spit them back on a test won't be too helpful in your life. Really knowing something will.
See: Focus, Successful at School

Keys

Keys to the car, keys to your house, keys to life. We use keys to turn things on (to start the engine) or to open a lock (on the front door). A key is a tool. The three keys to being successful are calm, confidence, and focus. These aren't just nice ideas, they are tools. Nine of them. Use these keys to get you started when you've stalled. Use these keys to open up possibility for yourself.
See: Calm, Confidence, Focus

Kindness

Means being friendly, generous, and considerate. We speak of "random acts of kindness" when we mean doing something for someone else, whether we know them or not. Try it out sometime. It's a real blessing for the other person and for you. And be kind to yourself. When you're a teen you can be very hard on yourself for doing or saying or thinking something. "What an idiot I am" isn't going to help you. Try, "What can I learn from that?" It's a much more kind way to go.
See: Confidence

Learning

Your learning goes on everywhere, all the time, not just in school. Whether you're on a bus, or at a job, or walking on the street or out in nature, keep your eyes and ears open to what's going on around you. We learn by doing. The ancient Chinese proverb tells us, "I hear and I forget, I see and I remember, I do and I understand." Focus on *doing*. Your learning depends on your actions.
See: Focus

Listening

Good listening requires paying attention. Whether you're listening to a teacher, a friend, a parent, or to your own inner voice, you have to train yourself to listen, otherwise your mind drifts off in a thousand directions. Listening, especially to the voice of your spirit, is the first step in taking the right action. Learn to distinguish that voice, the one that is giving you unfailingly helpful direction, from all the others. Some people call that the voice of their highest self, or of God. Whatever you call it, it's there 24-7-365. Stay tuned to that frequency.
See: Focus

Looks

Shorthand for physical appearance. Everybody's got "a look." Don't make a big deal about yours. Make the best of what you've got. "A look" can also be the way a person uses his glare to intimidate someone else as in, "Eunice's mother gave her a look." You don't like it when your parents try to intimidate you with hard-to-interpret or frightening non-verbal behavior like a "look." Consider that in your relationships with your friends and seek to give them supportive, encouraging looks.
See: Confidence, Calm

Mess

Clean up after yourself. And I don't mean just your room. If you've made a mess in a relationship, or in your work at school, clean it up. No one is paid to be your maid or butler (unless your parents have a lot of money and someone actually *is* paid to be your maid or butler). The world is messy enough, don't make it more so.

Music

Music is one of the great forms of human expression. It is universal because it is tied into human emotions, expressing joy, sadness, rage, serenity, and more. Notice how many different kinds of music there are all over our planet and even in one culture. Find music that expresses something meaningful to you. It doesn't have to have words. But remember: what's music to your ears may be bothersome noise to someone else. Don't be judgmental (see above) about what others are listening to. Put on your headphones.
See: Calm, Confident, Focus

Moderation

The opposite of excess. Can you eat one bowl of ice cream instead of taking a spoon to the whole pint? Can you play video games for twenty minutes instead of staying up for hours? The answer is "yes" to both questions. Moderation is best when practiced as a response to your own inner voice. Often we don't like to listen to or follow that voice (see "Listening" above), but wait instead for someone else to rein us in, like a parent or teacher, and then we resist them. ("No more ice cream for you!") Excess leads to problems, including addiction; moderation leads to balance.
See: Calm, Focus

New

We often use "new" to describe objects as in "a new car," "a new bike," "a new dress." In a culture as obsessed with "new" as ours, I like to think of "new" as something already existing but perceived for the first time, like "I had a new insight," or "The sweet smell of that rose was new to me." This suggests an openness, particularly to sensory experiences that take place when our minds are more rooted in the present.
See: Calm (sensing)

Negativity

Negativity can be toxic when it is darkly critical or pessimistic ("I won't pass this test. I'm just a loser"). It can also color how you see other people ("Sam is a loser"). Negative in mathematics is taking away, minus-ing, subtracting.

When you are negative, you are taking away from the possibilities inherent in any given moment of any particular person. Negative people look on the dark side and stay there. There's a lot about the world and the people in it, including yourself, that could work better. Instead of putting your attention on what doesn't work, focus on what does and how to improve it. Then take the actions necessary to move in that direction.

See: Focus

Never

"Never say never," is a wise directive. "Never" closes a door and seals it shut, leaving you in the dark part of your mind. Always keep the doors open to possibility. Use words such as, "possibly" and "perhaps." When someone tells you, "It will never happen," you can respond by saying, "I really don't know," or "It hasn't happened *yet.*"

See: Focus

Observing

Everyone has a part of themselves that observes what they're doing while they're doing it. This observer is often called "The Witness" (see "Witness" below). It can help you be more conscious of what you are doing when you are doing it. In that way you won't necessarily repeat old unproductive habits. "Observing" is also used in spiritual contexts when we observe rites and rituals, like observing the Sabbath, or observing silence. The practices help us break old habits and perceptions by taking us out of our normal routine and giving us the space to quietly observe.

Options

Options are choices. If you have an unproductive habit—procrastination, spending money unwisely, stretching the truth—no matter how ingrained it is, at the moment of action you still have options: you can choose to repeat the old habit once again, or you can choose to act in a different, productive direction. People who are addicted (alcohol, drugs, negative thinking) do not believe they have options. They believe they "are" that way. One of the daily, moment-by-moment, important parts of life where we always have options is in how we perceive a situation. You can see things in more than one way, including yourself. Don't get stuck. Always consider your options.

Overwhelmed

When you're buried beneath a mountain of homework you can feel overwhelmed. That quickly snowballs into feeling hopeless and defeated. Feeling overwhelmed doesn't suddenly happen. You can actually catch it before it gets to that point. Take homework, for example: if you start doing your homework, in a focused way with planned breaks, when you get home from school, you are not going to feel overwhelmed later. Sure, there might be a pile of it, but feeling overwhelmed comes more from sitting under the pile until midnight rather than doing something about it much earlier in the evening. If you start feeling overwhelmed, use the tools, all nine of them.
See Calm, Confidence, Focus

Personality

Personality is the combination of characteristics that form your distinctive character. Some schools of thought say we actually have several different personalities and we are choosing, consciously or not, at any given moment, which one we're going to project: like your happy personality, your sad one, your thoughtful one, or careless one. Imagine having a vase of roses—it's one vase, but if you turn it around you're going to see all kinds of different aspects of the roses. Your personality is like that: one you, but different aspects. This is not multiple personality disorder, which is a serious mental illness (when a person loses herself in different identities which can compete with and even harm one another).

Puberty

This is the name given to the time when your body is changing from being a child to a young adult. Hormones are pumping, sexual feelings are rising, pre-menstrual cramps are tormenting, voice changes can be embarrassing, pubic hair is sprouting, and so is your height. Since I was a teenager, I've never liked the sound of the word "puberty." I think it's a weird word. Whatever you call it, you have to simply accept that your body is changing. It doesn't matter how you feel about it. You might wish sometimes it wasn't happening (see *Wishing* below), but it is. Accept it. Enjoy it ("Are you kidding Dr. B?"). Find a friend and talk about what's going on with each of you and every other person your age.

Prison

Sometimes people, especially teens, feel like their bodies and minds are like a prison. They feel like they are locked into a body they don't like ("I'm too skinny . . . fat . . . short . . . tall") and locked into their negative thought patterns ("My life is a mess. It will never change!"). A prison is a place where people are held as a punishment for crimes they have committed. But (more than likely), you haven't committed a crime, so why lock yourself away in your self-negativity? For every "bad" or "wrong" thing you find in yourself, if you shift your attention you will see a completely different image: that you are a person who is capable of being happy, of loving and being loved. Have you ever been in an actual prison? It is a most gruesome, depressing place. Everything is taken away from prisoners—all their rights and their freedom to make choices. Look around you: the only thing you're locked into are your own habitual thoughts, feelings, and actions. Feelings, thoughts, and actions change all the time. You have many gifts in your life. Don't keep punishing yourself by staying locked into your negativity. Talk to someone who cares about you: a parent, a friend, a counselor, or a clergyman. Be grateful for what you have. The key to your freedom is love.
See: Confidence, Chapter thirteen

Pornography

Pornography is printed or visual material containing explicit descriptions or displays of sexual activity. It isn't about love or beauty or caring intimacy. It's about getting off. It reduces sex to something mechanical and impersonal and ultimately exploitative. Stay away from it. It acts like a drug, particularly because of its ready availability on the Internet. If you are looking at porn, you're probably being secretive about it (you don't want anyone to know), and likely you have all kinds of natural questions about sex. Find someone you can talk with about it, your parents, a counselor, a trusted friend, or a clergyman. A good friend of mine is a nurse in a high school. Many students come to talk with her about sex. Find someone like that, someone you can trust who will really listen and give you good feedback and helpful information.
See: Calm, Confidence, Focus, Chapter thirteen

Phones

As the entire world moves to communicating via mobile devices, how you deal with your phone turns out to be an important issue. Some teens and adults I know are positively addicted to their smart phones. They never let them out of their hands and are checking them constantly. If you're doing that, my big issue is that you are splitting your attention between what's in front of you and what's on your phone screen. You're not really present. You think you're multitasking, but that is a truly cooked-up, meaningless term. It suggests you are doing a lot of things at once. In actuality, you're flipping, in rapid succession, from one task to another and then back again. "Multi-cycling" would be much more accurate. Stop spinning your wheels and start *really* doing one thing at a time. How about *really* paying attention to the person standing right in front of you?

Questions

As you know by now, I'm a strong advocate of you asking questions. Why? Having a question can mean either that you want to know, or that you have a doubt about something you've heard or read. To me, questions are the mark of a curious, active, wanting-to-be-connected mind. Some adults don't like when young people ask too many questions because kids are generally prone to telling the truth before they realize that the truth is disturbing to many adults. When I was a young child I asked a lot of questions. So much was wondrous to me then ("How big is the sun?"), and so much didn't make sense ("Why is Mommy crying again?"). When I was very little, three or four years old, and I asked questions, and people smiled and said, "He's so cute!" A couple of years later, they said, "He's so smart!" And when I got a bit older, they weren't smiling anymore. Their eyes narrowed and they said, "Can't he go outside and play?" Ask questions. If someone is disturbed by your questions, then ask someone who isn't.

Quiet Time

Everybody needs quiet time, including you. "Quiet time" can mean anything from a five minute break in studying to a whole day off. Why is this important? Your nervous system has two parts: the sympathetic and parasympathetic. The first amps you up to pay attention and do stuff, the other calms you down. When you don't calm down—when you don't have quiet time—you are like a light switch that's stuck in the "on" position. Your light will burn out. Train yourself to take short and long breaks when you are studying. Rest your eyes occasionally when you are taking an exam. The world's great religions discovered thousands of years ago that taking a break is essential for reconnecting with what's really important: our health and well-being and other people in our lives. In some traditions it's called the Sabbath. This weekly break connects you to your spirit, to what really matters. It's like pressing a big restart button each week. Whatever you call that day or time, you need it. We all do.

Queer

This word has had quite a history. It started out meaning strange or odd ("He had a queer feeling that someone was hiding in the closet"), and then it started being applied, in a derogatory way, to homosexual men ("He's queer!" meaning, "He's *in* the closet). Then it got adopted by men who came out of the closet, who use it to defuse its negative connotation and as a sign of their solidarity ("Queer rights!"). It's like "gay," which years ago meant happy, carefree, and light. The point here is that language changes, and hopefully limited viewpoints also change so we can all be more accepting of each other.

Responsibility

Responsibility usually means a thing that one is required to do as part of a role or a job or legal obligation. A teacher of mine once defined it as "the ability to respond." I like that. I think that as you go through your teenage years you can cultivate the ability to respond to many different situations and people, which you'll have to do soon as you enter the job market or go to college. I think it's good for you to have more responsibilities: take on more tasks, keep your word, pitch in. As I said earlier in the book, if you want people to treat you like an adult then act like one. A *responsible* one.
See: *Focus, Confidence, Chapter thirteen*

Restraint

Restraint is related to moderation (see *Moderation* above), but different. Restraint is what you practice on the inside to help you to be more moderate in your choices and actions. Remember Topher, in the last chapter, who couldn't stop eating that second bowl of ice cream? When he learned to practice restraint he ate the dessert in moderation (one bowl only). Practicing restraint means using the Focus tools.

See: Focus, Chapter thirteen

Religion

If you are a Christian, Buddhist, Jew, Muslim, or member of any other religion (unofficially, there are twenty-two major world religions), you have a set of principles and practices that your religion proscribes for a healthy life—physically, mentally, and spiritually. This can be very helpful to some people because they join a path that many others have trod before them. If you don't feel a particular connection to a personal God or gods, or believe in religion at all, you still must come to terms, at somepoint in your life, with defining and practicing "right living" for yourself. What does it mean to you to live in a healthy, compassionate way? Similarly, belief in a particular religion doesn't ensure you will live properly. Only you can determine that by your goals, choices, and actions.

See: Focus, Chapter thirteen

Safe Sex

"Safe sex" means engaging in sexual activity in which people take precautions to protect themselves against unwanted pregnancy and sexually transmitted diseases. I have worked with many people, teens included, who have not practiced safe sex and then went on to suffer grave consequences: getting pregnant or contracting HIV. They thought, "I know what I'm doing," when they obviously did not, or "It'll never happen to me" but obviously it did. Do not take risks sexually. If you need to learn specifically what "safe sex" means, go on the web and find out. Now, before you get involved with anyone else.

Sex in Relationships

As you mature, your increased interest in sex will be a normal part of growing up. Sex always involves intimacy and vulnerability and a whole array of feelings. You need to be sensitive to your own feelings and needs and give equal weight to what the other person feels and needs. Without that kind of caring, sex can be selfish and lead to consequences like guilt, pregnancy, disease, and depression. Your questions and feelings about sex in relationships are very

natural and expected at this time in your life. For perspective and advice, I encourage you to talk to a parent, counselor, minister, priest, or rabbi to learn more about what kind of sexual relationships can bring joy to your life.
See: Calm, Confidence, Focus

Sexuality

Accept your sexuality, whatever it is. Whether you are gay, straight, lesbian, bisexual, or transgender, that's who you are. Enjoy your life. If someone makes you feel wrong about who you are, talk to someone who accepts you. It's natural to want to experiment with your sexuality. If you do, do it safely and with respect for the other person and for yourself. There is plenty of support for you out there. You are not alone.
See: Confident, Calm, Focus, Chapter thirteen

Suicide

When things are going very badly in your life, thoughts of "ending it all" may come up. You may feel like you just want to stop the noise and check out. If these thoughts persist, or they build into a plan, then it's much more serious and you need help. Depression at that stage feels overwhelming, that your life has become intolerable, the noise in your head too extreme, that no one really understands you, that you are a burden to everyone, and it would be better off if you are not around. I can tell you, from working with people who have had family members or close friends commit suicide, and myself having two friends who did, that committing suicide is not a solution. Its consequences are completely and unalterably devastating for everyone left behind. No matter how bad you feel, no matter how isolated you've become, there is always help and things will always change. Reach out to a friend, a parent, a teacher, a priest or rabbi, and God. Tell someone. Their heart will open to you. If there's no one you know to talk with, you can a suicide hotline. There is someone there, 24-7-365, to talk with you.
See: Calm, Confidence, Focus, Chapter thirteen

Texting

Here's the most important rule for texting: just text. Don't drive and text or talk and text or do-whatever-and-text. Just text. Texting while driving is dangerous and illegal. Texting while you're talking to someone else is rude. Rule two: be careful what you text. Once you've hit "Send," it's out there and you have no control over where it goes or what happens to it. "Sexting"—sending sexually explicit photographs of children and teenagers—is considered child pornography under the law and is a federal offense.

Trust

Let's look at two definitions of trust: (1) accepting the truth of a statement without evidence or investigation; and (2) to have faith or confidence in someone or something. If you want people, like your parents, to trust you (definition #2), you must do things that will engender their trust. You must show them that you are worthy of it, through your actions, not just your words. If you make an agreement with them or anyone, then keep the agreement. Otherwise you're asking them to simply accept whatever you say with nothing backing it up (definition #1). Most people are not going to do that. In other words, be trustworthy. You also need to trust yourself: that you will be able to handle challenging situations when they come up, whether at school or at home. This happens only by experience, as we learn to trust an "inner guidance" that we are all receiving, all the time, to do what's right.
See: Confidence, Chapter thirteen

Tension

We usually use "tension" to mean mental or emotional strain. In physics it's the state of forces acting in opposition to each other. This is what's actually happening when you say, "I'm so tense." Parts of you are pulling against one another. One part knows she needs to stay home and finish her homework; the other wants to hang out with friends. Neither is wrong, but the strain of pulling in two different directions creates tension. You can also feel tense physically because you are holding your muscles tight. Again, you are working against the force of gravity. Let go of the opposition and relax the tension. Stay in the present.

Trials

Life is full of trials that challenge your endurance and forbearance. "Forbearance" is an underused word these days. It means "patient self-control; restraint and tolerance." I decided to use "Trials" here instead of "Tests" because tests, especially the kind we have in school, are one kind of trial. In athletics, trials determine the selection of players eligible for a team. The three players on "Team You" are your body, mind, and spirit. They are undergoing trials all the time so they can consistently step up and work together as your winning team.

Universe

Do you know that the sun is one million times the size of the earth? And that our galaxy is one of a *billion* galaxies? The universe—all existing matter and space considered as a whole—is believed to be ten billion light years in diameter and is still expanding since its creation in the Big Bang about thirteen billion years ago. When I pause for a moment to open up my imagination to the vastness of the universe, I get unstuck from the tiny world of my "problems." Try it some time: open up to the bigger picture.
See: Chapter thirteen

Understanding

When you understand something you "get" it. You should understand what you are learning in school, not just memorize it. Real learning requires doing something, getting involved with the material. (See *Learning* above.) There's another meaning to "understanding," which is "a sympathetic awareness or tolerance, especially for people and beliefs different than our own." Cultivate your understanding of the ways other people are different than you.
See: Chapter thirteen

Video Games

There is a very addictive aspect to video games, and the creators and marketers of these games know that. They want you to keep playing, to knock out more opponents, to get more points, and to buy more video games. Video games can be great for developing your hand-eye coordination and quickening

your reflexes. So can riding a bike. I'd love to see more video games that require you to think, to reason, and to make ethical choices.
See: Restraint, Moderation

Violence

Any behavior that involves physical force that's intended to hurt, damage, or kill someone or something is violent. Many video games push violence as a contest if not a sport. This is deeply troubling. It is neither. Violence is deeply harmful to the victim and the perpetrator. We are living in a time when violence is becoming more common: a crazed gunman walking into a school and killing a score of children and teachers or armies bombing innocent people. We are also violent when we hurt or damage ourselves through addictions or unproductive habits that affect our health and well-being. Your life, and everyone else's, is a gift. Treasure it.
See: Focus, Chapter thirteen

Volunteering

If you have never had the experience of giving your energy and time to a worthy cause, I highly recommend that you do it soon. By serving a purpose greater than yourself, you will receive benefits beyond being paid. However you volunteer—reading storybooks to children in a hospital, sitting with an elderly person in a nursing home and asking them to tell you stories from their lives, working in a soup kitchen—you are doing a great service.
See: Chapter thirteen

Weight

For a culture as obsessed with being slim as ours is, we should put our time, energy, and money into eating healthy food and exercising regularly. Obesity is a major problem across America. It comes not just from bad eating habits but from loneliness and the need to be comforted. Strive for a deeper connection between people and the spirit that connects us, instead of your stomach and fast food.
See: Focus, Chapter thirteen

Wishing

In fairy tales, when the main characters are granted three wishes they usually ask for fortune, immortality, and a fabulous place to live. While I wish I had those, too, I'd rather wish for something that would make the world a better place. I wish people were more tolerant, giving, supportive, and accepting of themselves and others. What's your wish for humankind? What are you doing to make that happen?

See: Chapter thirteen

Witness

A witness to an event, who is a neutral bystander, someone who is taking in what's happening but is not part of it. In many spiritual traditions, people strive to develop "witness consciousness": an awareness of what you are doing and thinking, as if you were standing outside yourself watching what's going on. This gives you perspective. Do that now: as you are reading this sentence, see part of you taking three steps back and witnessing this event, seeing you reading and thinking. Being the witness to yourself will help you be more conscious of what you are doing when you are doing it. In that way you won't necessarily repeat old unproductive habits. Say you feel anxious about a test. Instead of spiraling into a panic attack you witness yourself getting tense and having fearful thoughts. At that moment you can choose to take another direction:you can use the Calming tools. Suddenly, your thoughts and feelings aren't as intense as they were a moment ago. You feel less stuck in them because you're observing yourself. Witness consciousness gives you distance to see things as they are and take a productive action.

See: Focus, Wishing, Chapter thirteen

X Marks the Spot

In large part, this book is about how to stay focused and the benefits that focus brings. In any activity there's going to be an "X," the "spot" to which you direct your attention if you want to score and if you want to win. In basketball it's the hoop, on a math test it's solving the problem, in a relationship it's clear, honest communication. "X marks the spot" is the goal. Keep your eyes on the prize. The prize is you being successful.

See: Focus

Xenophobia

The dictionary definition of this little-used word is "an intense or irrational dislike or fear of people from other countries." As the world continues to shrink and the oneness of our planet is more and more evident, an irrational dislike of people in other countries is not only backward, it's self-destructive. I recently heard about students in New Hampshire friending their counterparts in the Amazon jungle via Skype and Facebook. We need to let go of our fears and realize our partnership with every other person on this planet. We are, after all, one people.

See: Chapter thirteen

X-ray Vision

Some teens expect that others, particularly their parents, can intuit or somehow "know" what they are thinking or feeling. When they're angry or hurt and they shut down, they expect that others can read their minds and hearts. I don't know anyone who has x-ray vision. If something bothers you speak up. Don't expect someone to know how you are feeling. They're pretty preoccupied with themselves.

See: Chapter five

Youth

The expression "You're only young once," is partly true. Age-wise, yes, you're never going to be sixteen again. But your spirit is ageless, ever youthful. My great aunt Rachel passed away last year at age 105. She was vibrant and healthy until she had a massive stroke and passed away. Once I asked her, "Rachel, what's your secret to living such a long life?" She looked at me and said one word, "Love." Youth, youthfulness, and love go together.

See: Chapter thirteen

Yawning

When you yawn you're either tired or bored, or both. When I teach the people I coach the Calming tools, particularly breathing, many start to yawn uncontrollably. It's so rare for them to calm down, that just doing it gets them in touch with how driven and exhausted they are. One high energy high school junior actually fell asleep in my office as she calmed herself down. If you're yawning because you're bored, you might check out what's causing the boredom. You could say, "The teacher, of course!" But even with non-animated, seemingly disengaged teachers, you can stay engaged if you put your mind to it. Put your mind to it.

See: Focus

YouTube

There's a lot of good stuff on YouTube. And also a lot of junk. If you have something to share it's a great vehicle. I would advise coming up with something that other people could benefit from or be inspired by: something you and your friends did in the community; interviews that you do with special people in your family or circle of friends. We don't need more bad videos. We need uplifting stuff.

See Chapter thirteen

Zombie

I've never met one, but I'm open to it.

Zeal

When you have great energy or enthusiasm pursuing a cause or an objective, you've got zeal. If you were wildly passionate, you'd be called a "zealot." If you *really* didn't like that your best friend was going out with your old girlfriend, you'd be zealous.

See: Focus

Zone

This is the best place to be: in the Zone. When your stress is just enough to get your motor humming, you can perform—in any arena of your life—in a very focused, seemingly effortless and painless way. Of course it takes a lot of patience, perseverance, and persistence to get there, but the rewards are great: you have a sense of purpose and fulfillment. You can achieve your dreams. I've based my work for the last forty-four years on the science of being in the Zone, and I can tell you it works. BTW: now the term *zoning out* should have more meaning for you.

See: Focus, Chapter thirteen

CHAPTER 12

Give This Chapter
to Your Parents

If you like, you can read it too.

Appreciating You

I am sitting in India, in an airport waiting room. Next to me is a young couple with their children: an infant in a traveling stroller, and a little boy who is about five. The baby is crying loudly, and the boy is running around in circles yelling. The parents are clearly exhausted, on the edge of exasperation, and doing what they can to keep it together. I look at them with great compassion. I close my eyes and send them a prayer, a blessing that I hope will last for the next twenty years.

I salute you, as a parent, for the enormous responsibility you have taken on. Next to, and perhaps more than, classroom teachers, parents are grossly underappreciated, over-worked, and under-paid. I want you to know how greatly I admire and respect your commitment to parenting your teen.

I also want to appreciate your teen for reading this book and following the instruction to give you this chapter. By receiving it you are showing your interest in your child. I hope that these pages will give you food for thought and perhaps stimulate conversation between you and your teen.

Stress and
Your Performance as a Parent

In this book I've laid out a model for successful performance. As a performance psychologist for more than thirty-five years, I've coached people in high-stress/

high performance occupations to give them the tools they need to succeed. These people include professional athletes, school principals, actors, dentists, lawyers, opera singers, and politicians. I don't work on their technical skills (I don't know how to fill a tooth, or handle a lacrosse stick, or hit a high C), but rather I show them how to build a strong foundation for success, in every field, by learning to be calm, confident, and focused. For me the word "performance" isn't limited to what happens on stage or the ballfield, but rather it encompasses every area of human endeavor: how we perform as people, whatever it is we are doing. In this book I've written about how teenagers, like your child, can be successful at whatever they are doing by becoming more calm, confident, and focused.

After decades of clinical work, research, and teaching, I've found that staying calm, remaining confident, and staying focused are at the core of living a healthy, balanced, and fulfilling life. To me "success" means "fulfillment." It's not about having a larger income or a bigger house. Those things are nice but they never brought anyone true stability and happiness, which are more the result of inner states that endure rather than outer circumstances which are always changing.

You are welcome to read through this book to appreciate, first-hand, what this model is about and what your child has been reading. I encourage you to do this for three reasons: (1) you will gain insight into your child and the challenges he or she is facing as a teen; (2) it might stimulate discussion between you and your child about their challenges and the perspective offered in this book; and (3) you will be able to self-reflect. In other words, how calm, confident, and focused are *you*? The last is particularly helpful when we want or expect our child to do or be something we are not.

Specifically, are you wanting or expecting your child to be calm, confident, and focused when you are challenged—as we all are—in those areas yourself?

In the first chapters of this book I introduce the well-researched, scientific relationship between stress and performance. Too much or too little stress hurts performance; just the right amount of stress helps create optimal performance. This is true in any human endeavor. It's as true for physicians as it is for mothers; it's as true for CEOs as it is for teens. Think about it; it's not rocket science. As a parent, if you're stressed out, your performance is going to be compromised. You may act impulsively and scream at your child, you may doubt your parenting decisions, you may become distracted from taking care of the things you need to attend to on a moment-by-moment basis. In other words, too much stress and you won't be calm, confident, and focused. I say this with full awareness that sometimes we all "lose it" and that occasional screaming, self-doubting, and distraction do not in themselves constitute "bad" parenting. They are part of living. The question is how often do we lose it? And what do we do to recover and learn from what we've done?

If you are interested, you might want to complete the performance inventory on pages 31–32. This will give you a read on how calm, confident, and focused you are and which of those areas you might give more attention. You can find the information in the corresponding chapters in this book. Everyone will benefit.

Over the years I've seen how parental stress can contribute to, if not underlie, a child's stress. In this section I am going to ask you some challenging personal questions that relate to stress—your own and your child's. You can greatly help your child and yourself by honest self-reflection as you read through the next few pages.

Are You Contributing to Your Child's Stress?

There are basically four categories of what I call unhelpful parent behavior. As you look at the list below, see if there are any you identify with right away. You can go directly to that subsection (below the chart) or continue reading through.

YOU COMPARE YOUR CHILD WITH OTHERS	Do you compare your child's performance to a sibling's ("Your sister never had trouble with this."), or to yourself ("When I was in school I loved math.")?
YOU HAVE UNREALISTIC EXPECTATIONS FOR YOUR CHILD	Do you think your child is an unrecognized genius, or much smarter than everyone else seems to think or believe?
YOUR SELF-ESTEEM IS AFFECTED BY YOUR CHILD'S PERFORMANCE	Do you think your child's test performance is a reflection of your parenting? Is your real reason for wanting him to do well because it means other people will think you are a good parent? Do you want your child to be successful because you underachieved as a child and don't want her to repeat your story?

YOU WANT TO MICRO-MANAGE YOUR CHILD. YOU HAVE A HARD TIME LETTING GO	Do you believe the only way your child will stay on track is if you are constantly hovering over him, making sure every "t" is crossed and every "i" is dotted? When your child was younger were you a "helicopter" parent? Did you intervene on his behalf with teachers, coaches, and other kids? And now, as he's about to leave the nest, are you finding it hard to let go?
YOU HAVE A "SUCK IT UP" ATTITUDE	Do you believe life is to be endured and we are we meant to suffer?

Are You Comparing Your Child to Others?

Do you ever say to your child, "I don't understand why you find chemistry so hard. Your brother sailed right through this stuff," or "Your friend Ginny loves sports. Why don't you?" or "I was really into geometry when I was your age, what's the matter with you?" Comparisons like these send a message that you don't understand her or care about her; she is going to feel belittled and humiliated. You are making a situation that is already emotional even worse. Comparing her to a sibling, a classmate, or yourself just makes her feel as if she's naturally stupid and inept and no matter how hard she tries, she'll never measure up. What else can she conclude when you tell her it was easy for others? As I state in chapter six ("How to Remain Confident"), comparison is a trap, ensnaring you in an emotional tangle. The comparison takes the attention off the actual stress-producing aspect of the test and onto issues of self-esteem and love, so the child cannot address the real obstacle. The best thing to do is to focus on what is going on with her and what *she* needs, not on what anyone else is doing or has done. Go out of your way to ask your child questions so you can understand her needs. Say, "Tell me what you find difficult and what can I do to help you?"

Do You Have Unrealistic Expectations for Your Child?

Sometimes parents idealize their children and see them as mini superheroes capable of doing just about anything. But what happens if yours doesn't show an aptitude for a subject you think he should excel in, or if he doesn't like a sport that you think he should enjoy? What do you do when he under-performs? Some parents start blaming the teacher or the material or coach because it is hard for them to see their child as anything less than a little genius or star performer. This mentality gets in the way of seeing him for who he is. It is hard to see that he may not be the star in the way that you want him to be. Every parent wants the best for his or her child. And so should you. You are his greatest advocate and most enduring source of support. But you cannot be genuinely helpful unless you encourage him in a realistic way by recognizing his true strengths *and* weaknesses. You have to acknowledge and—this is harder—accept the things he likes and the things he doesn't, and be honest about his possibilities *and* limitations.

Do You Think Your Child's Performance Is a Reflection of Your Parenting?

Some parents believe that when their child fails a test or receives a sub-par report card, or doesn't score a goal in the big game, or flubs a music performance, that it makes it look as if the parents aren't doing their job. "What kind of parents let their child fail? Don't they make them study? Aren't they paying attention?" On the other hand, a straight-A report card or a stellar performance on stage seem to broadcast that the parents are putting in a sterling effort. In either case, you are tying your child's performance to your own self-esteem. This type of thinking isn't helpful to either of you.

If your child performs poorly on a test or in another area of his life it doesn't necessarily mean you have done a bad job as a mother or a father. It could just mean your child needs some help—either with the content or with performance issues. If you confuse your child's performance with *your* self-esteem you are making the issue personal and emotionally charged, which only elevates the stress levels. This is further complicated when the parent performed poorly in school and now has unresolved issues of shame, anger, or guilt. If you have difficulty separating out your child's performance from your own self-esteem or from your own performance as a child, you can avail yourself of different forms of support such as parenting books, online help, peer counseling (talking with other parents), or professional therapy.

Are You Micromanaging Your Child? Are You Finding it Hard to Let Go?

Sometimes a well-meaning parent, wanting their child to succeed, will always be hovering close by to make sure everything is done, and done right. This can extend to constant intervening with people who work with the child: the teacher, coach, parents of the child's friends. The term "helicopter parent" is a fairly recent addition to the lexicon of child rearing. While it is natural to want the best for your child, the very best is to give your child room to grow. It's hard to watch him make a mistake, or make the wrong choice, but true learning and growth come only through personal action. If you micromanaged your child and those around him when he was younger, you may have permanently affixed training wheels to your kid's bicycle, psychologically speaking. In other words, he may have become dependent on you and will have a hard time finding and maintaining his own balance to move ahead. This situation becomes compounded as your child matures through high school and needs to separate himself from you, and you from him. As he leaves high school he is about to strike off on his own. Letting go can be an extremely difficult challenge for some parents. (When I left for college my mother had another baby!)

If your tendency has been to over-intervene with your child or on her behalf, I would recommend you read chapter seven: "How to Stay Focused." First, clarify your goal as a parent. I suggest it is to provide a safe and healthy environment where your child can learn by doing, and grow in their own, unique way. Become aware when you feel the urge to jump in and take over for your child. At that moment use the tools: Stop! Ask yourself, "Is my intervening here supporting my goal?" Listen to your inner voice, which will direct you to take actions consistent with your goal. Calm down. Let your child take responsibility for himself. And finally, fulfill the direction of the voice by giving your child the space he needs. Stand back, observe, and, if it helps you, pray.

Do You Have a "Suck It Up" Attitude toward Challenges?

Often parents think that kids today have it way easier than they should. I've heard people say, "When I took the SAT, they didn't let *me* in the exam room with a calculator." They seem to think the calculator ought to alleviate all their child's woes and he should now skate to success. When a kid is stressed out over a test—in school or in life—some parents just don't understand it, and they don't offer a lot of empathy. "I had to suck it up, so should Billy." The problem with this attitude is that it might have floated in your day but times have changed. When you were your child's age you probably did what you were told ("suck it up"). Kids today are more aware of stress. While we all—children included—have many challenges to face, telling your child to just "suck it up" painfully disregards the very real struggle he is having and ought to be learning how to deal with. If you support him instead of demeaning his struggle, not only will you help him with the challenges he's facing, but you'll give him the tools to handle other stressful situations throughout his life.

The Effect of Marital Problems

I'd like to tell you a story about a teenager I am working with. I'll call her Ally. She is fourteen, very bright and personable, and also quite troubled. She doesn't keep up with her work at school, "forgets" when she has a test, occasionally cuts herself with a razor blade, and has been caught experimenting with drugs and alcohol. Her parents are afraid she's also having unprotected sex. Mom and Dad appear to be a model couple. They are in their mid-thirties, bright and highly successful. While they make a big effort to appear that they get along, their marriage is a minefield of disharmony. When I first talked with them, I could see the deep cracks in their foundation: in the way they shot pointy looks at each other; how their tones of voice became more strained when they referred to one another; and how they differed widely in their views of their daughter's behavior, subtly (and sometimes not so subtly) blaming the other for the trouble.

For Mom, Ally has "some problems" but is basically "fine." She calls her daughter "a normal teenager." For Dad, Ally is "messing up" and a constant source of concern. When I started working with Ally, I could see that though she was troubled with anxiety, depression, and distraction, she was, at heart, a good kid, and that her "troubles" were actually a way of saying to the world, "My situation at home is really tense and I am hurting." As I worked with her it became clear to me that Dad's obsessive concern about her was really his deflected desire to fix his wife. In other words, rather than put the focus of attention where it needed to be (on the marital relationship) it shifted to the child: *she* became the problem.

In over thirty-five years of practice as a psychologist, I have seen this situation repeated many times. It is always painful to witness. A troubled teenager is brought in with a slew of problems, but the major problem is actually in the relationship between two parents. Classical family therapy theory says that the "identified patient" (the child) may actually be the healthiest one in the family system because she is not covering things up. The "problem" is showing up *through her*. Yet when the child *becomes* the problem, everyone's concern is then locked onto her. The problem gets diagnosed, labeled (ADHD, depression, etc.) and then treated (therapy, special needs classes, medication), but the real problem goes untreated. I have had parents pull their child out of treatment when I insisted that *they* get help.

A marital relationship is complex and can, over time, like any relationship, become painfully knotted up. So much so that loosening the knot and sorting out the threads, and starting over—which may involve separation or divorce—seems too painful and complicated. If you are in this situation I strongly encourage you to do three things: (1) admit it, first to yourself and then to someone you trust; (2) seek professional help. I think that getting objective professional help is a must, either through counseling for yourself or for you and your spouse or partner; and (3) be honest with your children. Children have finely tuned antennae for what is going on with their parents, individually and together. I have found that it is much better to tell a child what is happening ("Your mother and I are having a hard time and are getting help") rather than let them imagine what is going on or what might happen. Invariably, kids imagine the worst, which usually includes thinking that *they* are the cause of the problem, and they can become very fearful or depressed about an imagined outcome ("What will happen to Mom, or Dad, or us?"). This is way too big a burden to put on your child. Children are not the cause of marital problems. Take responsibility for yourselves and get the help you need.

Your Focus: Be the Best Parent You Can Be

Who teaches you how to be an effective parent? No one. Human learning is a process that starts with imitation. For better or for worse, you learned about parenting from your parents and the way they treated you. I'd bet that at some point as a child or teenager you thought, *If I ever have children I'll never act the way my mom (or dad) is acting!* And here you are, many years later, doing the same thing with your children, and you think, "My goodness, have I turned into my mother? Have I become my father?" Sigmund Freud affirmed that we *repeat until we remember*. This means that imitation becomes habit, and if we want to change our habits—in this case as parents—we need to look *consciously* at what we are doing, right now, and see how our actions and thoughts affect our children, and how we can change the future by not repeating the past.

If you've scanned through this book, you can see that I've been working with your teen in exactly the same way: helping them cultivate their awareness about how their unproductive habits create stress and negatively affect their performance; and then giving them tools to use to reduce their stress and improve their performance in all areas of their lives.

You can do the same thing. You can learn to be more calm, confident, and focused.

First, learn how to calm yourself down. As a parent, it is very easy to pick up on what your child feels and start feeling the same way yourself. (Also, of course, you have your own adult problems to cope with.) If your child is anxious, or sad, or angry you may quickly begin feeling the same thing even if you were feeling quite calm just moments before. In psychology we call this an "induced reaction"—you are induced into your child's state. This is a very human response, especially with people who are close with one another like parent and child. You increase your chances of reducing your child's stress if you learn how to keep yourself calm no matter what is going on with them. The material in chapter five, "How to Calm Down," will show you how to do this.

Next, be confident yourself. Your child's self-doubt might induce you into thinking you haven't done a good job as a parent. Not necessarily true! Everyone has issues, but don't confuse yours with your child's. She is a separate entity. You will be a better resource for her if you work on keeping your own self-confidence strong without being arrogant. Using the tools in chapter six will help you do that.

Finally, how focused are you? If you have clear goals and minimize distraction, you can be a good role model for your child. She can see the effects for herself. The different sections on focus in chapter seven can help you strengthen this part of yourself. Remember: cultivating good work habits is ultimately something children should learn to do for themselves because they see the positive results and feel good about having accomplished a goal. Though you may have to encourage and mentor them through this process, they are doing the work so that *they* can go on to lead a more fulfilling life. They can't motivate themselves to work hard just because you want them to. The long-out-of-favor proverb, "Virtue is its own reward," needs to return.

Summing Up, Moving On

The teenage years are an enormous challenge—for everyone. It is a time of true individuation and separation, which can be hard for your teen and for you. If you and your teen use the tools to be more calm, confident, and focused these years don't have to be a fight or burdensome. You and your teen can collaborate to reach his or her goals. You are not competing with your child, nor can you live through him or her. Your main job is to see, clearly, the person emerging in your son or daughter. They have their own lives and each one has his or her own story.

Understand and appreciate the stresses your child is facing on a daily basis. Are you aware of the different requirements in all of your child's classes, or what's going on socially with them? Try saying to your child: "Help me understand what you're finding so difficult in math," or "It must be hard when your friends aren't including you in their plans." This lets her know that you are there for her.

Don't judge your child and don't interpret his behavior. Judging your child means saying something to him that sounds critical: "You are not good at science because you don't use your head and think logically." Interpreting sounds like you are his therapist: "I think the reason you're not doing well is that you expect people to do everything for you." (This is also judgmental.) These approaches don't work. Judgments and interpretations are triggers that make teens turn off to their parents.

Determine whether your child is as confident as he appears. Do you ever have the feeling that he is always trying to put up a good "front"—that he wants it to appear as if everything is all right when it really isn't? If you suspect this, acknowledge his desire to do well, and also affirm that sometimes having some self-doubt is normal. It's better to bring these doubts to the light of day than to pretend they don't exist. Ultimately the self-doubt will undermine his self-confidence.

If your child is under-performing in school or in another area of her life, does she express an interest in improving? Ask her if she would like to work with a coach or tutor, or a program as presented in this book.

Look out for increasing disconnection and possibly depression. Listen to what your child is saying about particular subjects or about school in general. If he is complaining a lot, is mostly dissatisfied and is rarely happy when he comes home from school, it is likely a sign that he is growing more and more disengaged and is possibly even depressed. There might be something that he does enjoy at school but overlooks. If you find out what that is you may begin to understand what fires him up. Could it be certain subject matter? A particular teacher? Answering these questions will also give you a clue as to why your child is disconnecting in other subjects. If he seems to have lost all interest in school and in other parts of his life, he may be depressed and need a different level of support, such as professional counseling.

As a parent you are your child's chief role model. Remembering again that no one is perfect and that we all make mistakes, expecting your child to be more calm, confident, and focused will only really work if you are making the same effort in your own life. Don't expect them to be someone you are not willing to work towards yourself.

I recommend you read chapter nine, "Happy at Home." In it you will find some guidelines for clear communication. If your child commits herself to putting the principles and tools into practice, I think it's reasonable, and compassionate, to meet them halfway, to do your part as a growing human being, and as your child's principal role model.

Whoever said growing—or life—is easy? It's not. It's an ongoing resolution of opposites: good and bad; happy and sad; easy and hard. And through all of this is the day-to-day, and sometimes moment-by-moment, challenge to be one's best self. Being calm, confident, and focused sets the stage for the best possible human performance at home and at work. And it never stops: the challenge to grow is as true for the child as it is for the teenager as it is for you, the parent, as it is for me, the psychologist. When you meet your own challenges this way, every moment is a building block to a fulfilling, successful life, and an opportunity to inspire your teen.

CHAPTER 13

On Your Path

Do you recall how this book began? The first sentence read, "You've got a lot going on." And so you do. Your days are filled with school, home, friends, sports, music, volunteering in your community, and much, much more. Yet with all of these different situations and activities and all of the different people in your life, there is one constant, and that is *you*. Whatever you're doing, whomever you're with, wherever you are, you are still *you*.

As you've seen throughout the book, my coaching is geared to giving you the tools you need to be successful in any situation, with any person, wherever you find yourself. As I said initially, I can't teach you to how to solve differential equations in math, or kick a soccer ball, or play the trumpet. There are many good teachers, coaches, and books that can give you what you need for that. What I've given you is what you need, *on the inside*, to succeed at anything you want to do. I've given you the tools to be calm, confident, and focused in any situation you face.

Do you ever wonder, *what's the purpose of life*? I certainly do. This question is one of the biggest mysteries we human beings face. I don't pretend to know The Answer, but I am going to tell you what I believe, which is this:

> *The purpose of life is to face every challenge, every test, as an opportunity to be and to become the person you are meant to be—your highest self— so you can make your own unique contribution to the world we live in.*

As a teenager, you are in a major transition in your life. You are moving from being a child to being a young adult. In the past you've been fully dependent on others and now you're becoming more independent. In this transition time, you are probably noticing how much your life is filled with highs and lows and surprises and shocks. You may wish that only good things would happen to you, but you now realize that's a recipe for frustration and disappointment. Everyone's life has challenges, tests and stresses. Every day things happen to you—and to me—that are hard, that we wish weren't happening, and yet, every day we have to deal with whatever comes our way, whether it's a tough chemistry test, a hurt friend, an opposing football team, a frustrated parent, a struggling economy, or a war in some part of the world.

You may well wonder, "Shouldn't life be easier?" The answer is, simply, "No." I'm sorry if that disappoints or frustrates you, but no one gets to decide how life *should* be. Even a person who has lots of money or is in a position of power can't stop an earthquake, or cancer, or being hit by a car, or losing someone close to them. Life simply *is* whatever it is, and we all have to deal with it. If you really want to grow, if you really want to lead a successful, fulfilling life, you will learn to face every situation, no matter how "good" or how "bad" it seems to you, in a way that is more calm, confident, and focused.

In the fourth century a rabbi and sage named Hillel asked three questions:

> If I am not for myself, who will be for me?
> If I am only for myself, then what am I?
> And if not now, when?

What do these questions have to do with you?

If I Am Not for Myself, Who Will Be for Me?

When you were a young child, your parents or guardians anticipated your needs, cared for you when you were sick, and protected you from harm. But now, as you are growing, you realize that everyone has to look after himself or herself, and you have to do that, too. You realize that the world doesn't owe you anything, and that if you're going to get on in this life you basically have to learn to take care of yourself. You have to keep your body calm, your mind confident, and your spirit focused. Hillel is saying that if you don't do this, who, really, is going to do this for you?

But Hillel's first question goes further. If you are truly "for" yourself then you are your own advocate, your own supporter, your own close friend. You want the best for yourself and you work for that consistently. True, you have people in your life who care about you and love you, but the primary responsibility for your well-being is yours.

I recently started working with a seventeen-year-old who has been suspended from school repeatedly for drinking and smoking pot. When we first met he explained his behavior by saying, "I just want to feel good," which meant, to him, that he thought he *was* taking care of himself by getting high. I'm sure you can see the fallacy in his thinking and how it played out in his actions and their consequences. To me, "taking care of yourself" means building productive habits that keep you healthy in body, mind, and spirit. Doing the "right" thing—like staying home and doing your homework instead of going to the movies—might not feel great in the moment, but I can guarantee you that the long-term effect of consistently making choices that keep you focused, confident, and calm is that your life will work better and better, and you will be fulfilled and successful.

If I Am Only for Myself, What Am I?

No one's life exists in a vacuum. Each of us is part of a much larger whole—a network—that extends to our family, our town or city, and ultimately to our world. You're more than an isolated, self-involved entity-unto-yourself. You are a contributing member of the world in which you, and I, and your parents, and your siblings, and your fellow students and your teachers, and your politicians, and everyone all around the planet is part of. Being only "for yourself" is selfish and also self-defeating, because *we need one another* to create a sustainable world in which everyone has the opportunity to flourish.

Notice that Hillel says, "If I am only for myself, *what* am I?" He doesn't say "*who* am I?"

"What" suggests a function, a purpose. Since each of us is part of a whole, every one of us has a function, which is to support that whole. We do that first by being healthy ourselves, because then we can contribute to our fullest.

A couple of years ago I was crossing the street in New York City and was run over by a speeding taxicab that jumped a red light. I suffered severe multiple fractures and was in a hospital bed for two months. This horribly traumatic event ended up having a positive effect. As I lay there, immobilized and in pain, I knew I had a goal: I was going to get myself strong and healthy, whatever it took. So I worked diligently, on a daily basis, with the doctors and physical therapists, even when I didn't feel like it. As I got stronger I realized that getting myself healthy was not the end goal. The goal of being healthy was that I would be able to better serve other people.

And so I offer this to you: as you work on developing productive habits so that you can be and become your best, brightest, and true self, you will be building yourself to contribute more fully to your family, your community, and the world we all live in. No matter what you end up doing when you "grow up", whether you become a mother, an engineer, a doctor, a janitor, an athlete, or a business person, you will make that contribution with more awareness, more connection, and more positive effect if you start laying that foundation now.

There's another, less obvious, facet of Hillel's second question, *If I am only for myself, what am I?* and that is this: you are not alone. Just as you are part of and are supporting the great network of humankind, that network is also supporting you. At times you might feel isolated and lonely, like no one understands you or cares what you are going through. Sometimes these moments come often in your teenage years. This is the phase of life when you're in the midst of a lot of physical, mental, and spiritual upheaval. At times like these you need to remember that *everyone* has times like this and that when you are in the midst of difficulty, you can connect to someone who will care and who will be there to give you a supporting hand.

Fortunately for you, reaching out is now easy through the web, where you have instant access to unlimited resources and potential help 24-7-365. Initially, I considered having a "resource list" at the end of this book. My publisher asked a very wide circle of people for their recommendations as to what to include: websites, articles, blog posts, and books on subjects such as bullying, suicide prevention, pregnancy, sexuality, addiction, and more. What came back was illuminating: the list of responses was very long and hugely varied. It made the point that there is so much readily available to you *right now* if you need help. Rather than sit alone in your room feeling cut off and helpless, turn on your computer, open up your browser, and type in whatever support might be helpful to you right now. Instantly, you'll get an almost endless list. If I chose "the best" suggestions it well might not be exactly what you are looking for. I want you to be empowered to look for what *you* need right now.

And if Not Now, When?

This brings us to Hillel's third question: what are you doing *right now* to take care of yourself and to be and become a contributing member of the world? Say you had a math test earlier today and you didn't study for it as well as you could have and so your stress level was up and your score was down. Now you're thinking "I know I could have been more calm, confident, and focused when I prepared for the test and took it. I'll make sure I am the next time a math test rolls around."

As you can tell, this thinking is partly in the past ("I should have . . . ") and partly in the future ("I will . . . "). It isn't in the present, the now. This is very common in human thinking: we've got one leg in the past where we're feeling regret or guilt about what we could have or should have done, and one leg in the future, where we're worried about what's coming.

And yet, what's really happening is the now, the present. This is what Hillel is pointing out to us: *If not now, when?* The past is gone. We can't do anything about it. The future hasn't happened yet, so why worry? Right now you're here, in this moment. This is the field of action, the opportunity for you to make choices.

So what do you choose right now? Do you choose to do what will keep you healthy and strong, to keep building and strengthening your foundation of being calm, confident, and focused, and by so doing be able to serve others in a fuller, richer way? Or do you choose to do things that weaken your foundation and thereby hurt yourself and limit your ability to be a full contributor to your community and our world?

Your choices are driven by your habits. If your habits are unproductive, you're going to end up with unsatisfactory results. If you have a habit of cramming for exams then you can bet the next time an exam comes along, you'll cram again, you'll be stressed out again, and your scores will be lower, again. Sure, you can do it by cramming—you've done it many times before— but to what effect and at what cost? It's the same with any habit.

When you have a disagreement with your parent and your habit is to shut down, stomp away, and slam the door, you will only get more disagreement, dissatisfaction, anger, and resentment.

You always have opportunities to do things differently *right now.* That's what Hillel means: *If not now, when?* And *now* has a powerful effect on what's coming. In every moment you are making choices that will determine your future. If you are filling up the present with regrets about the past or fears of the future you are, literally, missing the point. If you are doing things, right now, that hurt yourself or others, your future is always going to be a big cleanup operation or rescue mission.

Recently I began a correspondence with a young man who is in prison. He was caught driving drunk three times and because his state has a three strikes law, he was put away for seven years. Seven *years.* I went to visit him in the prison. I'd never been in one before. It was gruesome. Stark, bleak, and very depressing. When you're in prison everything is taken away from you. Every choice is made for you. You have, literally, no freedom. Being there was a profound experience for me. I realized that while most of us don't live in a prison building, we are, in fact, imprisoned by our own unproductive habits. When you do the same thing over and over that hurts yourself or others—no matter how small an action that is—you are chained to that habit. You are living with the illusion that you are free, but you're really not.

So what is freedom, if it's not the opportunity to choose? It's actually the state that comes from making the right choices. As you choose to act in ways that are more calm, confident, and focused you won't be locked up in your old, unproductive habits. You will be entering each moment with the freedom to create the future you truly want, the one you deeply dream about.

Life moves on. It isn't waiting for you to change. Challenges come, for every one of us, many times a day. And every challenge is a chance to cultivate a new, productive habit. Now you have the tools to do that. If you are tensing up, you can calm yourself down. If you are doubting your abilities, you can rebuild your self-confidence. If you don't have a goal or you are distracted from reaching the one you have, you can get yourself back on track by becoming focused.

I think that one of the big revelations of the teenage years is that you realize what you are doing is *your choice*. To be free is to stay on a path where each step is a sound, healthy, productive choice. Freedom isn't something that's happening outside of you. It's an inner condition. It's the way you see your world. It's the way you decide to do *this* instead of *that*. Right now. It's the way you are creating your own future. Right now.

Think of your life as a story. Each one of us is living a story and no real story is without trials for its characters. Without the tests of life, no one would become stronger, more skillful, or more experienced. Think of the sword that has to be thrust in the fire and then pounded into shape before it can become perfect. Without going through this process, it is merely a hunk of metal. The fire and the shaping help it to become what it is meant to be.

None of us comes out of the box already formed. It is our experiences and the way we deal with them that shape us into what we are. In life, we have to perform every day, and every challenge—whether it is in school or at home, with family or with friends—is a chance to strengthen yourself, to perform at your best and to grow. Challenges are the stuff that actually help us become and be who we are meant to be.

We don't choose the challenges we are given in life, but we do choose how we are going to face them. Are we going to have a miserable experience, crumble under the pressure, run away, or avoid challenges altogether? Or are we going to find the strength and inner resources to rise to them and fully actualize our potential? When a close friend of mine received a terminal cancer diagnosis she didn't fold up and just die. The doctor told her that her life was going to be an uphill climb. My friend responded by saying, "Well, we'll just have to walk uphill. " And we all joined her on that path.

That's what life is—a path that runs up hills and down, with challenges and trials and tests popping up around every turn. We can't possibly know what they will be, but each and every one challenges us to grow so that we can fully be, individually and collectively, the people we are meant to be and support each other to do so along the way.

Video games are a huge part of our culture, but even though they're only fantasy, in a strange way they are a reflection of life. Have you ever wondered about their huge, worldwide appeal? Their origin is in the arcade games of the '50s, where you slid into a darkened booth, dropped your ten cents into a coin slot, and sat behind a steering wheel. A movie would come on a small screen and suddenly you were steering a car on a road that became, by turns, easy and perilous, relaxed and eventful, exhilarating and scary. How you dealt with the bumps and potholes, the incursions and intrusions, determined your score.

Video games are often designed to simulate life. We are racing around curves and meeting the expected and unexpected on a daily basis. Your ability to be a "winner" in the game of life is determined by how you maneuver the turns and deal with the surprises. Are you prepared? Do you have confidence? Do you have the strength and courage to take on whatever comes?

It's one thing to be at home manipulating your joystick or pressing buttons or pushing your mouse through the twists and turns on a TV screen or a computer or mobile device. It's quite another to stay in control when someone you know is dying, or you have an autistic sibling, or your mom lost her job, or you are determined to stop your addiction to drugs or alcohol.

The present—the path you are on right now—continuously affords you the chance to move ahead in a new, productive, and successful way. Every challenge takes place in the present. To succeed, you have to interrupt and redirect any old habit that keeps you disconnected and adds stress, and put a new habit in its place, one that connects you to your true path, which is to be your best, highest, most successful self. Only then can you move ahead. Instead of staying stuck, you have a chance, whenever you choose, to actually change your life by being more calm, confident, and focused.

Step up to the plate. This is *your* life.

"*Many, many men have been just as troubled morally and spiritually as you are right now. Happily, some of them kept records of their troubles. You'll learn from them—if you want to. Just as someday, if you have something to offer, someone will learn something from you. It's a beautiful, reciprocal arrangement. And it isn't education. It's history. It's poetry.*"

The Catcher in the Rye,
J. D. Salinger

ABOUT THE AUTHOR

Ben Bernstein, Ph.D., is a psychologist, educator, and performance coach.

His client list includes athletes, actors, students, opera singers, business executives, attorneys, and dentists. He is the author of *Test Success!* (Spark Avenue, 2013), and has received major grants for his work from the American and Canadian governments. His model for successful performance is currently used in schools, universities, programs for underserved college-bound youth, and in prisons.

Dr. Bernstein was the first director of improvisation at Robert Redford's Sundance Institute in Utah, and has directed theater at The Juilliard School and the Australian National Academy of Dramatic Art. He created and produced original musicals and films with adolescent and young adult psychiatric patients in the US and Australia, and is a member of the creative team for the new animated television show *Didi Lightful*.

Born in Brooklyn, New York, Bernstein is a graduate of Bowdoin College, with a doctorate from the University of Toronto and a master's degree in music composition from Mills College. He has coached his three younger siblings in their successful artistic careers: sister Didi Conn, Frenchy in *Grease* and Stacy in *Shining Time Station*; brother Andrew, head photographer for the NBA; and youngest brother Richard, in leading roles at the Metropolitan Opera. His wife, Suk Wah, is a novelist. The couple lives in the Bay Area, California.

For questions or comments, please contact Dr. Bernstein at
teensguideforsuccess@gmail.com.

ABOUT THE PUBLISHER

Familius was founded in 2012 with the intent to align the founders' love of publishing and family with the digital publishing renaissance which occurred simultaneously with the Great Recession. The founders believe that the traditional family is the basic unit of society, and that a society is only as strong as the families that create it.

Familius' mission is to help families be happy. We invite you to participate with us in strengthening your family by being part of the Familius family. Go to www.familius.com to subscribe and receive information about our books, articles, and videos.

Website: www.familius.com

Facebook: www.facebook.com/paterfamilius

Twitter: @paterfamilius1 and @familiustalk

Pinterest: www.pinterest.com/familius

helping families be happy

CPSIA information can be obtained at www.ICGtesting.com
Printed in the USA
BVOW081319230413

318899BV00002B/3/P